STUDY ABROAD MADE SIMPLE

A complete guide for supporting international university applications

NEIL ROSCOE

Study Abroad Made Simple

This first edition published in 2026 by Trotman, an imprint of Trotman Indigo Publishing Ltd, 18e Charles Street, Bath BA1 1HX.

© Trotman Indigo Publishing Ltd 2026

Author: Neil Roscoe

British Library Cataloguing in Publication Data
A catalogue record for this book is available from the British Library.

Paperback ISBN 978-1-911724-79-7
eISBN 978-1-911724-80-3

All rights reserved. This book is sold subject to the condition that it shall not, by way of trade or otherwise, be lent, resold, hired out or otherwise circulated without the publisher's prior written consent in any form of binding or cover other than that in which it is published and without a similar condition including this condition being imposed on the subsequent purchaser. No part of this publication may be reproduced, stored in a retrieval system or transmitted in any form or by any means, electronic and mechanical, photocopying, recording or otherwise without prior permission of Trotman Indigo Publishing.

Every effort has been made to trace copyright holders and to obtain their permission for the use of copyright material. The publisher apologises for any errors or omissions, and would be grateful to be notified of any corrections that should be incorporated in future editions of this book.

The authorised representative in the EEA is Easy Access System Europe Oü (EAS), Mustamäe tee 50, 10621 Tallinn, Estonia.

Printed and bound in the UK by 4edge Ltd.

All details in this book were correct at the time of going to press. To keep up to date with all the latest news and updates and to access the online resources that accompany this book, use this QR code or visit www.trotman.co.uk/pages/study-abroad-made-simple-resources

Dedication

For Linda and Ivan, my parents — with love and gratitude.

Contents

List of figures and tables	vii
Acknowledgements	ix
About the author	xi
Preface	xii
Introduction	xiv
1| An introduction to global university applications	1
2| University guidance in a global context	12
3| Guiding the way: Decoding subject choices and careers	25
4| Making your application stand out	38
5| Applications and standardised testing	51
6| The European perspective	62
7| Exploring the East: Applying to Asia, New Zealand and Australia	78
8| Transatlantic aspirations: Applying to the US and Canada	92
9| Alternative pathways: Broadening horizons beyond the traditional route	111
10| Navigating costs and financial aid	127
Conclusion: A journey shared, a future shaped	143

List of figures and tables

Figures

1.1	Top destinations for international students (2025)	3
1.2	QS World University Rankings – top 10 universities (2026)	7
3.1	A typical curriculum model	28
10.1	Average tuition fee *v.* typical subsidy/aid by country (GBP)	133
10.2	Typical annual undergraduate tuition fees for international students (GBP)	134

Tables

1.1	Global university application systems and deadlines	6
3.1	Degree requirements	35
5.1	Standardised tests	56
6.1	An overview of European applications	75
7.1	Asia and Australasia compared	88
9.1	Overall comparison – commercial *v.* volunteer schemes	116
9.2	Summary of gap year programmes	117
10.1	Comparative overview: Tuition and living costs by country	129
10.2	Work hour limits by country	137

Acknowledgements

Sincere thanks to Gary Woodward, writer, coach and former deputy director of careers at the London School of Economics and Political Science, and to Nicola Cattini, editor at Trotman, for their invaluable support in proofreading the draft manuscript and offering constructive suggestions. Their expertise and attention to detail have greatly enhanced the clarity and consistency of this book.

About the author

Neil Roscoe is a university guidance counsellor, science teacher and education professional with a career spanning 30 years, including seven years working internationally. He is currently based in Thailand, in a school where he has served as both a counsellor and teacher. His international experience also includes time at a leading school in Shanghai, China.

In the UK, Neil has taught at schools in Sussex, including Ardingly College and Roedean, as well as in comprehensives in his early career. Over the last 15 years, he has also specialised in supporting students applying to higher education, with particular expertise in medicine and medically related courses. His background also includes leadership roles: as the Head of Education and Training at the Royal Society of Biology where he contributed articles to both of the Society's journals as well as other journals such as *Science in Parliament*.

Neil has also served as Chair of Governors at a school in London, reflecting his wider commitment to educational leadership. His writing experience includes the development of A level biology teaching resources and consultancy work in educational publishing. This blend of counselling, teaching, governance and writing experience underpins his ongoing commitment to guiding students towards successful university applications.

Preface

Education has always carried with it the promise of transformation. For many students, the opportunity to study beyond familiar borders – whether geographical, cultural or intellectual – is not only life-changing but life-defining. This book is written to provide the knowledge to support those who are considering, planning or navigating that journey: students looking to explore education across countries, systems and perspectives.

In thinking about the enduring value of international education, I have often returned to the vision of Rabindranath Tagore. His approach, striking in its originality, remains deeply resonant today.

In the early 20th century, when education in many parts of the world followed formal, exam-driven models, Tagore offered something different. Best known internationally as the first non-European to win the Nobel Prize for Literature, he was also a remarkable educational reformer. He believed that learning should be expansive, creative and deeply human – something that nourishes curiosity and brings people together across cultures.

In 1901, he founded a small school in rural Bengal, which he named *Santiniketan* – 'abode of peace'. Lessons took place under the open sky, and students were encouraged to learn through the arts, nature and dialogue rather than memorisation and repetition. Tagore's goal was not simply to instruct, but to inspire.

That philosophy grew into Visva-Bharati University, established in 1921 as a place where learning could cross boundaries. The name means 'India in the world', and its founding motto, *Yatra visvam bhavatyekanidam* – 'Where the world makes a home in a single nest' – spoke to its international outlook. Scholars and students from across Asia, Europe and North America came to take part in a shared academic and cultural life.

Courses were taught in multiple languages, with a curriculum that embraced art, science, agriculture, philosophy and literature. Learners from Japan, Germany, the UK and the US studied alongside their Indian peers. In every way, Visva-Bharati reflected Tagore's belief that education should be both locally rooted and globally engaged.

Beyond his own institution, Tagore travelled widely – visiting more than 30 countries to share his ideas on education, cultural understanding and peace. He formed lasting friendships with thinkers such as Albert Einstein and Romain Rolland, and was respected around the world for his commitment to what he called the 'unity of truth' – a belief that knowledge should unite, not divide.

In today's complex and fast-changing world, that message still holds true. Education that reaches across borders helps to develop not only knowledge, but perspective, resilience and a sense of shared responsibility.

Preface

This book aims to support students on that path. While its focus is practical – providing clear, up-to-date guidance on studying abroad – it also reflects a wider aspiration: to help shape learners who are confident, open-minded and ready to take part in a world that is increasingly connected.

Neil Roscoe
Bangkok, July 2025

Introduction

How to use this book and who is it for?

This book is designed to support advisers in delivering informed and effective guidance. It is primarily aimed at teachers and advisers working with UK-based students who are considering studying abroad. It will also be relevant to teachers in British international schools worldwide, parents supporting their children through international study decisions, and particularly to staff members taking on a guidance role for the first time.

To help the reader get the most from each chapter, the content is structured for clarity and ease of use. Each chapter includes:

- A summary of the key themes and topics that the chapter will cover, offering a clear overview and helping you quickly locate relevant sections.
- Case studies throughout, illustrating how key points play out in real-life scenarios with students and advisers and offering practical context.
- An adviser checklist towards the end of the chapter, providing prompts and reminders to support student guidance.
- Further information at the end of chapters, showing where to find additional resources and reading on the topics covered.

You can read the book sequentially or dip into chapters as needed. The structure and added features are designed to support both approaches, making this a flexible and practical resource.

Chapter overviews

Chapter 1: An introduction to global university applications. This chapter explains why more UK students are considering universities abroad, outlining key benefits and differences in global admissions systems. It introduces the idea of shifting international demand and highlights potential risks, particularly in the US.

Chapter 2: University guidance in a global context. This chapter offers a framework for supporting students pursuing international higher education, highlighting key differences from UCAS, including timelines and holistic admissions. It provides strategies for building strong profiles from Year 9, outlines best practices for managing references, and addresses how to navigate complex conversations with families.

Chapter 3: Guiding the way: Decoding subject choices and careers. This chapter supports advisers working with students in Years 8 to 11 as they make subject choices that shape future academic and career paths. It clarifies the difference between required and preferred subjects, introduces digital tools like Morrisby and

Unifrog, and emphasises open, student-led conversations that balance aspiration with wellbeing. It also highlights the value of transferable skills in an evolving global job market.

Chapter 4: Making your application stand out. This chapter explores how international universities assess applicants beyond grades and the adviser's role in guiding effective self-presentation. It offers practical advice on writing European letters of motivation and US essays, highlights the value of extracurricular and super curricular activities, and recommends enrichment tools to support academic exploration. The chapter also addresses the ethical use of AI in application writing, with strategies for ensuring authenticity.

Chapter 5: Applications and standardised testing. This chapter explains the role of standardised tests in global admissions and when UK students may need them. It covers key exams like the SAT, ACT and IELTS, compares requirements across major destinations, and outlines preparation strategies and timelines. It also explores test-optional policies, helping advisers support students in making informed decisions.

Chapter 6: The European perspective. This chapter explores the opportunities and challenges for UK students applying to European universities, highlighting key destinations, costs, admissions systems and language requirements. It covers practical matters such as visas, accommodation, and touches on work regulations, and offers adviser-focused guidance alongside trusted sources for up-to-date information.

Chapter 7: Exploring the East: Applying to Asia, New Zealand and Australia. This chapter examines university options in Asia, Australia and New Zealand, outlining how their admissions systems differ from UCAS. It explains academic requirements, including ATAR conversion and English-language tests and introduces TAFE colleges as a vocational route for BTEC students. The chapter also compares timelines and qualification recognition, offering practical guidance for advisers and parents on planning, documentation and cultural readiness.

Chapter 8: Transatlantic aspirations: Applying to the US and Canada. This chapter explores the academic and personal benefits of studying in the US or Canada, including liberal arts programmes and the idea of 'fit'. It explains the application process via platforms like Common App and OUAC, unpacks holistic admissions and guides advisers in helping students craft strong personal narratives. The chapter also clarifies how UK qualifications are translated and the key differences in terminology for UK applicants.

Chapter 9: Alternative pathways: Broadening horizons beyond the traditional route. This chapter explores non-traditional routes to higher education, including gap years, internships and study-abroad opportunities. It outlines the structure and benefits of UK degrees with a year abroad and provides guidance on planning both structured and self-sourced experiences. Advisers are supported with practical advice on funding, visas, safeguarding and sourcing placements, showing the lasting impact of global experiences to help make students 'work ready'.

Chapter 10: Navigating costs and financial aid This chapter breaks down the full cost of studying abroad, from tuition and living expenses to visas and hidden fees. It builds on country-specific information provided in earlier chapters and compares costs across major destinations. It outlines financial aid options including scholarships and clarifies student work rights by country. The chapter also explains visa requirements, proof of funds and fee categories to help families plan effectively and avoid financial surprises.

Online resources

There is a range of useful **online resources** that accompany this book, which can be accessed by scanning the QR code or visiting the web address at the start of this book.

Important note

This guide has been carefully researched to provide clear, accurate and up-to-date information to support advisers, teachers, parents and students. However, details such as tuition fees, entry requirements, visa rules, application systems and work entitlements can change at short notice.

We strongly recommend that students always check the latest information directly with official sources – including universities, government immigration services and trusted national agencies – before making any decisions or submitting applications.

Where possible, use the official websites listed throughout this book for the most reliable and up-to-date guidance.

1 An introduction to global university applications

This chapter will:

- Explain why international higher education is increasingly relevant to UK students.
- Highlight key advantages of studying abroad – academic, personal and financial.
- Outline how global admissions systems differ and where UK qualifications are accepted.
- Introduce the concept of global supply and demand in university admissions and how they can change depending on geopolitical variations.
- Provide a realistic overview of risks, especially in relation to studying in the US.

Introduction: Nadia's story

Nadia had ambitions to be a doctor ever since she was a small child. From an Irish Catholic family that had moved to the UK, her parents were supportive of her chosen career path. She studied A level Sciences and Maths at a sixth-form college in London. A diligent and hardworking student, she secured conditional offers from several Russell Group universities, including UCL.

When results day arrived that summer, her chemistry grade had slipped to a B. Before Nadia had even opened her results envelope, she had been rejected by both her firm and insurance choices. She was devastated. The college principal offered tissues and sympathy in his office, but the real turning point came later that day in a tearful meeting with her biology and chemistry teachers. They encouraged her to explore options beyond the UK – specifically, a university in Prague.

With some reluctance, she called the admissions office at Charles University. What she didn't yet know was that the institution – one of Europe's oldest and most respected – offered far more flexibility on entry grades than her UK choices. After an hour of redialling and a conversation with the university, she returned to the science lab, looking shocked.

'I need to book a flight to attend an interview,' she announced.

Nadia was offered a place. Thanks to her warm personality and clear commitment, she flourished. She went on to qualify in Medicine and was later admitted to the Royal

College of Surgeons. Today, she works as a surgical registrar at Croydon Hospital. She recently emailed her biology teacher, the author, to share the news – and to thank him and her chemistry teacher, Dr Spriggs, for encouraging her to take that life-changing step.

This case is an example of what can happen when advisers and teachers have good knowledge of the international higher education landscape. In the UK, Nadia's path seemed blocked. But overseas, doors remained open. Nadia became an exceptional doctor and has gone on to treat hundreds of UK-based patients. This book is written in the hope that there will be more Nadias – more students whose ambitions are realised, not limited, by the systems around them.

The many advantages of studying abroad

Studying abroad is not just an academic choice – it's a transformative personal journey. One of the most immediate advantages is exposure to different ways of thinking. Studying in a new cultural environment encourages intellectual curiosity and adaptability. Students are introduced to fresh academic perspectives, unfamiliar teaching methods and different ways of solving problems. This variety helps to develop independent learning skills and a global outlook – qualities that are increasingly valued in a competitive job market.

Living and studying abroad also builds confidence. For many students, it is their first time navigating life in a foreign country – opening a bank account, managing healthcare, finding accommodation and working with others from a diverse range of backgrounds. These challenges, while at times daunting, foster resilience and maturity.

Language is another key advantage. Even when studying in English, students often find that immersion in a different linguistic environment sharpens their communication skills and, in some cases, leads to fluency in a second or third language. This linguistic ability not only broadens personal horizons but also enhances future employment prospects.

There are financial benefits too. In certain countries – Germany and the Nordic nations, for example, tuition fees are low or non-existent, even for international students. Other countries, such as the Netherlands, offer high-quality degrees taught in English at a significantly lower cost than UK or US equivalents.

These financial incentives are more than anecdotal. A 2020 British Council study on transnational education found that cost savings, access to globally recognised degrees and improved employment prospects were among the leading motivations for students studying abroad. The report also noted that many students perceive international education as a strategic step towards building cross-cultural competence and gaining a competitive edge in the global job market (British Council, 2020). These findings reinforce the idea that studying abroad isn't just about affordability – it's about long-term opportunity.

Finally, an international education can help students stand out, whether they plan to build their career at home or abroad. Employers value graduates who can work with different cultures, adapt to new situations and bring a global outlook to their work.

1 An introduction to global university applications

For many students, the experience and connections made abroad can strengthen opportunities for years to come, wherever they choose to live and work.

Higher education: A global marketplace

Higher education is increasingly a global marketplace, and students – along with their families – are becoming more discerning in their choices. For UK-based students, there are numerous reasons to consider studying abroad, even if just for part of their degree: the chance to experience a different culture, the availability of English-taught courses, the opportunity to study in institutions with world-class reputations, and in some cases a significant reduction in fees or living costs.

Where are the top destinations globally?

International student mobility continues to evolve, with shifting trends reflecting changes in policy, demographics and global demand for higher education. Figure 1.1 shows the most popular destinations for international students at the post-secondary level in 2025, based on approximate shares of global enrolment. The US remains the leading host country, attracting about 20% of all international students, followed by Australia (15%), the UK (14%) and Canada (14%). Germany and France maintain strong appeal within Europe, while Japan, South Korea and China reflect growing interest in Asia. Ireland, though smaller in absolute numbers, continues to gain traction as an emerging hub for higher education.

FIGURE 1.1 Top destinations for international students (2025). Sources: IIE Open Doors Report; UNESCO Global Education Monitoring; Immigration, Refugees and Citizenship Canada (IRCC); Statistics Canada; HESA (UK); Australian Department of Education; national education agencies.

1. United States – 1,126,690 international students
2. Canada – approximately 800,000 international students
3. Australia – 853,045 international students
4. United Kingdom – 758,855 international students
5. Germany – 469,485 international students
6. France – 412,087 international students
7. China – over 200,000 international students
8. South Korea – 208,962 international students
9. Japan – 279,274 international students
10. Ireland – emerging as a leading hub for international students

A market shaped by supply and demand

Although higher education is now a truly global market, with diverse and often complex application systems, one key principle is common to all: supply and demand.

At its core, the university admissions landscape follows the same logic as any traditional market. When demand for a particular course or institution increases, and supply is limited, the cost of entry tends to rise. But unlike most economic models, the cost here isn't just financial – it's academic.

There are, effectively, two axes at play:

- Price – the financial cost of attending (fees – but often government regulated for some public institutions).
- Selectivity – the academic thresholds for entry.

Some institutions may charge higher tuition fees but offer flexible entry criteria. Others are academically selective but relatively affordable, particularly in parts of mainland Europe or Asia.

For example:

- A Pharmacy degree in the UK might require A*AA and cost up to £9,535 per year in tuition.
- A comparable course in the Czech Republic or Poland may accept slightly lower grades and charge considerably less – often with the option to study in English.

This dual model means students can consider which institutions best align with their academic profile, ambitions and financial circumstances. For advisers and teachers, understanding this framework is key to presenting realistic and inspiring options.

Global admissions systems and recognising UK qualifications

While application timelines vary, one reassuring constant is that most international systems recognise and accept A levels. In many countries – across Europe, the US and parts of Asia – students can apply before receiving final grades and may be made conditional offers based on teacher-predicted results.

However, some countries, such as Australia or Germany, require final certified grades before considering an application. This may necessitate a gap year or later application cycle.

University application systems around the world vary widely. In some countries, students apply directly to individual institutions, often by email or through an online form. In others, applications are submitted through centralised portals, which may involve service fees and set application deadlines. For example, students applying to Dutch universities typically use the Studielink platform; in the US, many institutions accept applications via the Common App or Coalition App; and in Australia, applications often go through state-based portals such as UAC (Universities Admissions Centre) in New South Wales. These systems differ not only in format but also in terms of documentation required, entry criteria and timelines. Each has its own quirks and

1 An introduction to global university applications

conventions, which will be explored in detail in the relevant country-specific chapters that follow.

BTEC qualifications and global admissions

It is important to note that recognition of vocational qualifications such as BTECs or T Levels varies by country, unlike in the UK where their acceptability is much greater, as they are essentially a British qualification. In the Netherlands, for example, the BTEC Level 3 National Extended Diploma (equivalent to 3 A levels) is considered comparable to the Dutch MBO level 4, granting access to universities of applied sciences (HBO). However, shorter BTEC qualifications (such as the subsidiary diploma) may not be sufficient for direct admission.

In other European countries, acceptance of BTECs depends on the subject and institution. Some may require additional documentation or foundation courses. In all cases, early communication with universities and, where necessary, formal credential evaluation is vital. Some institutions will not evaluate 'unusual' qualifications such as BTEC, unless an official application is submitted and paid for, in which case early applications are encouraged.

BTECs remain a valuable pathway, but their portability abroad is more limited than A levels. Individualised advice and early planning are key.

Global university application systems and deadlines: At a glance

Applying to universities around the world involves understanding a wide range of systems, deadlines and tuition costs. Table 1.1 (overleaf) summarises key information for advisers and students considering international study, highlighting typical deadlines (in approximate chronological order), average undergraduate fees (converted into GBP), and standard degree lengths.

Interpreting rankings — and seeing beyond them

QS World University Rankings are a common reference point for families exploring international options. These rankings are based on several indicators, including academic and employer reputation, staff-to-student ratios, international faculty numbers and research citations. While helpful as a broad comparison tool, they don't always reflect the quality of teaching, student experience or support. (Note: QS stands for Quacquarelli Symonds, named after its founder Nunzio Quacquarelli, and is the organisation behind the widely used QS World University Rankings).

Parents often place great importance on rankings, especially when evaluating unfamiliar institutions. Yet a sole focus on prestige can obscure a more vital question: *Is this the right fit for the student?*

As Malcolm Gladwell explores in his book *David and Goliath*, students placed in highly competitive and ranked academic environments may underperform

TABLE 1.1 Global university application systems and deadlines

Country/region	Application system	Typical deadlines	Average fee (approx., GBP)	Typical degree length
United Kingdom	UCAS	15 Oct (Oxbridge, Medicine), 14 Jan (main)	Up to £9,535/year (home students)	3 years (BA/BSc)
United States	Common App/Direct	1–15 Nov (early), 1 Jan (regular), rolling options	£20,000–£48,000/year	4 years (BA/BSc)
Hong Kong	JUPAS/Direct	Dec–Jan (JUPAS), Oct–May (direct/international entry)	£4,000–£14,000/year	4 years (BA/BSc)
Sweden	universityadmissions.se	15 Jan (autumn intake), mid-Aug (spring intake if offered)	Free (EU students); £7,700–£12,900/year (non-EU)	3 years (BA/BSc)
Germany	Uni-assist/Direct	15 Jan (summer intake), 15 Jul (winter intake)	Mostly free (£200–£500 admin fees)	3–3.5 years (BA/BSc)
Ireland	CAO	1 Feb (standard), 1 May (late application)	£2,600/year (EU students)	3–4 years (BA/BSc)
Singapore	Direct (e.g. NUS, NTU)	Jan–Mar (main intake), earlier for internationals	£14,800–£26,600/year	4 years (BA/BSc)
France	Parcoursup/Direct	Mar–Apr (public universities), varies for private	£2,400/year (public universities)	3 years (Licence)
Canada	OUAC/Direct	Dec–Mar (varies by province), Jan typical for Ontario	£12,000–£24,000/year	4 years (BA/BSc)
Czech Republic	Direct to institutions	Jan–May (for September start), earlier for Medicine	£4,000–£12,000/year (English-taught)	3–6 years (varies by field)
Spain	Direct/UNEDasiss	Jun (post-results), earlier for private institutions	£650–£2,150/year (public universities)	4 years (Grado)
Italy	Direct to institutions	May–Jul (non-EU applicants), varies by course	£860–£3,400/year (public)	3 years (BA/BSc)
Poland	Direct to institutions	Feb–Jul (varies by university)	£1,700–£5,200/year (English-taught)	3 years (BA/BSc)
Netherlands	Studielink	15 Jan (numerus fixus), 1 May (most courses)	£2,200/year	3 years (BA/BSc)
Australia	Direct/State systems	Oct–Dec (Semester 1), Jul (Semester 2)	£10,600–£24,000/year	3 years (BA/BSc)
New Zealand	Direct	Oct–Dec (February start), some July intakes	£10,800–£15,700/year	3 years (BA/BSc)

Note: All deadlines, tuition fee ranges and course lengths have been verified using the International Admissions Calendar 2024/25 and cross-checked against official university admissions portals, national education agencies and sector-standard sources, but it's always best to check the university in question's website.

1 An introduction to global university applications

– not because they lack talent or intelligence, but because of the psychological impact of constantly comparing themselves to high-achieving peers. He highlights research showing that students who rank lower in a top-tier institution often feel inadequate, even if they would have been top performers in a slightly less selective setting.

This sense of relative underperformance can lead to a loss of confidence, reduced motivation and, in some cases, a higher likelihood of dropping out. In contrast, students at less prestigious universities often thrive because they feel more capable and valued. Gladwell refers to this as the 'Big Fish-Small Pond' effect: being a strong performer in a smaller or less elite environment can lead to greater self-esteem, persistence and overall success. His findings challenge the assumption that more competitive always means better – and reinforce the idea that finding the right academic and social fit can be more important than prestige alone. Having said that, Figure 1.2 provides the latest QS rankings.

FIGURE 1.2 QS World University Rankings – top 10 universities (2026). Source: QS World University Rankings 2026. www.topuniversities.com/world-university-rankings [Accessed: 19 June 2025]

QS World University Rankings – top 10 universities (2026)

1. Massachusetts Institute of Technology (MIT), United States
2. Imperial College London, United Kingdom
3. Stanford University, United States
4. University of Oxford, United Kingdom
5. Harvard University, United States
6. University of Cambridge, United Kingdom
7. ETH Zurich – Swiss Federal Institute of Technology, Switzerland
8. National University of Singapore (NUS), Singapore
9. University College London (UCL), United Kingdom
10. California Institute of Technology (Caltech), United States

Shifting fortunes: Why UK universities are falling behind while Asia climbs

While rankings like those published by QS offer a snapshot of global academic prestige, they also reflect deeper, long-term shifts in funding, policy and research infrastructure. In recent years, several UK universities have slipped down the rankings, a change attributed in part to sustained under-investment in the higher education sector. Vivienne Stern, Chief Executive of Universities UK, has publicly cautioned that this trend will continue unless the government commits to a long-term financial settlement. With tuition fees effectively frozen and inflation steadily eroding their real value, many universities have been forced to reduce investment in teaching and research – a move that directly impacts international reputation and performance metrics.

By contrast, countries such as Singapore and China have made higher education a strategic priority. The National University of Singapore (NUS), now ranked 8th in the world, exemplifies how sustained investment and policy focus can elevate an institution's global standing. The latest QS analysis identifies Asia's upward momentum as a direct result of government-led funding initiatives, expanding research capacity and aggressive international recruitment strategies.

Visa policy is another factor reshaping global student flows. Tighter restrictions in the UK and US, including curtailed post-study work rights and limits on bringing dependants, have prompted some students to explore more welcoming alternatives. Asian universities, bolstered by both financial support and favourable immigration policies, are increasingly seen as attractive destinations for ambitious international students seeking both academic quality and long-term opportunities.

This global realignment underscores a vital point: rankings are not just reflections of past performance, but indicators of where resources, priorities and talent are heading. For advisers and families using this book to guide their university applications, understanding the structural and political forces behind ranking changes can offer essential context. It reminds us that choosing a university today means considering not just reputation, but also future-facing factors – like investment trends, policy environments and the long-term sustainability of an institution's global position. This perspective becomes especially relevant when it comes to weighing up application choices across different countries – an issue explored in the later section on selecting the best-fit destination.

Advising UK students on US immigration in 2025 and beyond: A shifting landscape

As the US undergoes renewed immigration reform under its second Trump administration, UK-based students considering US undergraduate study are navigating a more complex and uncertain environment. While UK passport holders remain broadly eligible for student visas, several recent changes have introduced new administrative hurdles, particularly for those with dual nationality or connections to countries currently under heightened scrutiny.

In June 2025, Executive Order 10949 reinstated a targeted travel ban affecting 12 specific countries. Although the UK is not among them, students with dual citizenship or family ties to restricted nations may face additional visa complications. These potential risks should be flagged early during the research and application stages, especially when advising students from globally diverse backgrounds.

Visa processing itself has become more rigorous. All F-1 and J-1 student visa applicants are now subject to enhanced screening measures, including the mandatory disclosure of social media accounts. From September 2025, most applicants must attend in-person interviews, reversing previous exemptions that had streamlined the process. As a result, students may encounter longer waiting times, more detailed questioning and heightened scrutiny of their digital presence. Even posts shared years earlier – particularly those expressing political views or criticism – may be reviewed and could influence visa outcomes.

In a small but growing number of cases, student visas have reportedly been delayed or revoked due to perceived political affiliations, with some decisions later overturned following legal challenges. While such incidents remain relatively uncommon, they point to a more cautious and unpredictable visa environment, particularly for students active in social or political discourse.

Additional administrative changes have also raised the financial and logistical barriers to studying in the US. A new 'visa integrity fee' of $250 was introduced in mid-2025, adding to already significant visa costs. While students from the UK may be exempt in some cases, the overall application burden is clearly increasing.

For students who remain committed to studying in the US, these challenges are not insurmountable – but they do require careful preparation and timely support. Institutions with strong international student services, experienced visa advisers and a demonstrated commitment to protecting international students will be especially important. Advisers should help students weigh not only academic and financial fit but also institutional capacity to support them through a shifting political and immigration landscape.

The US continues to offer a world-class education and a wide range of academic and cultural opportunities. But in the current climate, pursuing study there requires not only ambition and academic strength but resilience, foresight and the right guidance at every step.

Finding the right fit

When exploring options, students should be encouraged to reflect on factors beyond academic rank:

- Academic style – is the course theoretical or practical? Are there opportunities for interdisciplinary study? Is there one course of study or major and minors? Any possibility of additional short courses (electives), which gain credit?
- Teaching and support – what are class sizes like? What pastoral care or career guidance is in place?
- Work placements – are internships, sandwich courses or a year in industry available?
- Language – is the course taught in English? What language skills are needed for daily life?
- Environment – does the student prefer an urban campus or smaller town? Is it a city or suburban setting – the availability of public transport?
- Cost – what are the tuition fees and living costs? Are scholarships available? The possibility of gaining local fees (perhaps for dual nationals)?
- Outcomes – what do graduates go on to do? Are internships or placements integrated into the degree?

Advisers, parents and teachers play a crucial role in prompting these reflections. Tools such as Unifrog, BridgeU (see Chapter 3) and virtual campus tours can help students create meaningful shortlists. YouTube videos posted by actual students provide a good insight into what an institution is really like, aside from the official marketing reels. Ultimately, the goal is not just university admission, but *long-term success*.

A launchpad for personal growth

In an increasingly global university landscape, access to opportunity is no longer defined solely by borders or exam results. For students like Nadia – and for the thousands more weighing their next step – international higher education offers not just an academic destination, but a launchpad for personal growth and lifelong possibility. For advisers, the role is both empowering and essential: to demystify complex systems, to advocate when options appear closed and to illuminate the many paths still open. This book aims to equip you with the tools and confidence to do just that. In the chapters that follow, we'll explore how to navigate applications country by country – helping your students turn aspirations into achievable, exciting futures.

Adviser checklist

Understanding student motivations
- ☑ Ask why the student is considering studying abroad.
- ☑ Discuss personal, academic and career-related reasons.
- ☑ Highlight the long-term benefits, including independence and global employability.

Exploring study destinations
- ☑ Introduce a range of countries beyond the UK and US.
- ☑ Ensure students are aware where A levels and BTECs are accepted.
- ☑ Discuss which countries offer English-taught courses and how entry criteria vary.

Evaluating course and university fit
- ☑ Encourage students to look beyond rankings.
- ☑ Discuss academic style, teaching methods and support structures.
- ☑ Explore factors like campus location, cost of living and cultural environment.
- ☑ Explain the importance of choosing a place where the student will feel confident and supported.

Understanding application timelines
- ☑ Highlight key deadlines for major destinations.
- ☑ Explain differences in application systems (e.g. direct v. centralised).
- ☑ Emphasise the importance of early planning, especially for competitive or specialist courses.

1 An introduction to global university applications

Supporting non-A level students
- ☑ Clarify how BTECs and other vocational qualifications are viewed internationally.
- ☑ Advise on early communication with universities if qualifications are less commonly recognised.
- ☑ Suggest credential evaluation where necessary.

Signposting resources
- ☑ Point students to trusted platforms (e.g. Studielink, Common App, EducationUSA, Unifrog).
- ☑ Recommend virtual tours, student-created videos and university comparison tools.

Addressing risks and realities
- ☑ Provide up-to-date information on US visa and immigration changes.
- ☑ Discuss the need for careful documentation and preparation for international applications.
- ☑ Encourage students to have more than one country option if possible.

FURTHER INFORMATION

Studielink – www.studielink.nl

Common app – www.commonapp.org

Daad – www.daad.de/en

University admissions Sweden – www.universityadmissions.se

QS World University Rankings – www.topuniversities.com

Educationusa – www.educationusa.state.gov

US visa information – www.travel.state.gov

Nafsa – www.nafsa.org

Unifrog – www.unifrog.org

Nuffic (Dutch regulations) – www.nuffic.nl/en

ENIC-NARIC – www.enic-naric.net

2 University guidance in a global context

This chapter will:

- Provide a clear framework for supporting students who wish to pursue higher education outside the UK.
- Explain how international admissions processes differ from UCAS, including application timelines and holistic evaluation methods.
- Offer practical strategies for building long-term, competitive international profiles from Year 9 onward.
- Highlight key digital tools – such as Unifrog, BridgeU and Match – that support global guidance.
- Set out professional standards and practices for managing international references and documentation.
- Explore how to handle complex conversations with students and families, including disagreements over course choices.

Rethinking traditional guidance models

In an increasingly interconnected world, higher education has become a truly global enterprise. More and more students are looking beyond national borders in search of academic specialism, cultural enrichment and new personal and professional horizons. For UK-based schools and advisers, this means rethinking traditional guidance models and expanding their expertise to include systems, qualifications and expectations that extend far beyond UCAS.

This chapter provides a clear and practical framework for supporting students with international aspirations. From the US to Europe, Canada to Asia, we explore how university admissions differ from the UK model, what advisers need to know, and how to help students prepare over the long term. Alongside regional overviews and application timelines presented elsewhere in this book, this chapter offers insight into digital tools, best practice in counselling and the importance of developing a school-wide culture that supports global opportunities.

Key differences from UK admissions

For advisers familiar with UCAS, navigating international applications can feel like entering an entirely different world. While the UK system is centralised, relatively streamlined and places a strong emphasis on predicted grades and the personal statement, many other systems operate quite differently – placing greater weight on a student's broader profile, academic trajectory and personal engagement.

One of the most striking contrasts is the timeline. Applications to US universities often begin as early as the end of Year 12, with early deadlines in October or November of Year 13 – well ahead of the typical UK January deadline. Similarly, institutions in the Netherlands and elsewhere in Europe may use rolling admissions or staggered deadlines depending on subject and institution. This requires students to begin planning earlier and to stay organised across multiple systems.

Another key distinction is the nature of the application itself. In the UK, the personal statement is a focused, largely academic piece and references are written by advisers, heads of sixth form or tutors with teacher input. In contrast, US applications may require multiple essays, including personal narratives and university-specific supplements, as well as recommendations from individual subject teachers and a separate one from the school counsellor (usually the head of sixth form or tutor fulfils this role in the UK). Canadian applications vary by province, but some also include holistic elements or optional statements of interest.

Ultimately, the most important difference is philosophical. Whereas UK admissions tend to prioritise academic potential in a specific subject, many international systems – particularly in North America – adopt a more holistic view, considering extracurricular involvement, character, leadership and community engagement alongside academic metrics. This calls for early and sustained preparation, and for advisers to help students build a well-rounded and authentic profile over time.

What this means for UK schools

For UK schools and advisers, supporting international applications means going beyond traditional UCAS-focused advice and recognising the diversity within each student cohort. How this is approached will vary greatly depending on the type of school, its intake and the backgrounds of students and families. Many families with roots overseas may hope for their children to return to their home countries for higher education, while others look for specialist courses or new opportunities further afield to improve career prospects.

This makes it vital for advisers to really know their students and understand each family's context. Much of this insight comes through regular one-to-one meetings, where advisers can ask open questions about future plans and preferences. Lower down the school, simple surveys or questionnaires – for example, Google Forms completed by KS3 or KS4 students – can help build an early picture of students' global intentions and shape the guidance programme accordingly.

It is also part of the adviser's role to reassure families who may feel anxious about their child studying overseas. Well-informed guidance can help families see that international pathways are realistic, affordable and achievable when planned carefully.

In practice, many students may choose to apply through UCAS and also to a few universities abroad to keep their options open. Advisers should help students find the right balance: too few applications and they risk missing out; too many and the process can become time-consuming and stressful. A good rule of thumb is around five applications in total, counting the whole UCAS application as one. Advisers should also encourage students to be realistic about the number of countries they apply to, as each destination can have different deadlines and requirements. Personal statements written for UCAS can often be adapted into letters of motivation for European universities, which can save time and effort.

For schools themselves – and for a senior management team that may be fixated by Oxbridge or the Russell Group – sending students to top universities around the world is a powerful part of their marketing story. Highlighting successful international applications demonstrates a genuine global outlook and reassures families that the school is equipped to support a wide range of pathways, not just the domestic route.

Case study: A teacher writing their first US-style reference

Context

Mr East, a sixth-form economics teacher at a London academy, was asked to write a reference for a student applying to a US university. While confident writing UCAS-style comments, he had never written the narrative-style letter expected in the US.

Challenge

The teacher was unsure what tone to strike, how much personal insight to include, or how to format the reference. The deadline was tight, and the school's guidance team was already stretched with UCAS processing.

Adviser strategy

The school's careers adviser arranged a short lunchtime session for staff, walking through the structure and purpose of a US teacher recommendation. They provided a model letter, suggested sentence starters and a brief checklist to guide the writing process. The adviser also offered to proofread any references before submission.

Outcome

Mr East produced a strong reference that focused on the student's classroom contributions, personal growth and resilience. He later reported feeling more confident and volunteered to write references for future US applicants.

Five-year plan: A checklist for building a competitive international profile

Supporting students with international aspirations begins well before the final year of school. Competitive global universities – especially in systems that prioritise holistic admissions such as the US – expect to see evidence of long-term growth, commitment and breadth. Advisers can play a key role by helping students and families structure a five-year plan that prepares them academically and personally for success across multiple systems. While perhaps not as vital for a UK-only cohort, this longer-term view will also serve to support students focusing solely on UCAS and can generally be seen as good practice (e.g. by organisations such as UCAS, the Career Development Institute (CDI), the International Association for College Admission Counseling (International ACAC) and the Institute of International Education (IIE)). For some students, they may not be sure about their future pathway five years in advance of the time for applications, but it remains important to start considering their profile with a good spread of extracurricular activities well in advance. The specific degree subject can be finalised later. In order that advisers can target support where it is most needed, where possible, it's useful to have an idea early in a learner's secondary education which countries they are likely to be applying to.

Years 9-10: Early exploration and foundations

At this stage, students should begin exploring international pathways and considering what motivates them to study abroad. Encourage participation in school clubs, academic competitions and early volunteering or enrichment programmes. This is also the time to ensure students are making strong GCSE or equivalent subject choices to keep global options open – particularly for countries that favour breadth across sciences, maths and humanities – such as the Netherlands, where institutions like University College Utrecht encourage interdisciplinary study.

- Encourage engagement in extracurricular and super curricular activities (e.g. coding clubs, debating, extended reading or creative writing).
- Promote language study, which may support international mobility.
- Introduce early research into university systems and destination countries.

Year 11: First steps towards an international profile

This is a critical year for aligning students' academic and personal profiles with potential global destinations. It's also the right time to start discussing standardised testing if US, Canada or Asian universities are being considered.

- Support early SAT or ACT preparation, if relevant.
- Encourage participation in Model United Nations, Duke of Edinburgh Award or STEM summer schools.
- Introduce MOOCs or independent research projects (e.g. Coursera, FutureLearn). These are discussed more in future chapters.
- Help students start building a working CV or activities list.

Year 12: Depth, direction and decision-making

Students should now be actively building the strongest possible case for admissions. This includes continuing with academic challenges (e.g. EPQ, Olympiads), refining their extracurricular focus and beginning work on testing, essays and application strategies.

- Register for SAT, ACT, TMUA or language tests (IELTS/TOEFL) as appropriate.
- Begin essay writing (e.g. Common App personal statement, supplemental prompts).

- Narrow university lists and research institutional requirements and deadlines.
- Continue tracking skills and achievements using platforms like Unifrog or BridgeU.

Year 13: Applications and execution

In the final year, advisers play a pivotal role in managing deadlines, supporting references and helping students finalise and submit applications. This is also the time to monitor results, coordinate offers and advise on practical next steps.

- Finalise application portal sign up (Common App, OUAC, Studielink etc.).
- Submit test scores, transcripts, references and financial documents.
- Help students navigate scholarship or visa processes.
- Support offer comparisons and the decision-making processes.

Digital tools for global guidance

With students applying to an increasing number of destinations, digital platforms have become essential for managing the complexity of international applications. From course research and skills tracking to reference coordination and application timelines, tools like Unifrog and BridgeU offer advisers powerful ways to streamline support and personalise guidance.

Unifrog

Unifrog is widely used in UK and international schools to support career and university research. For globally minded students, its most valuable features include:

- Careers and subjects library: A searchable database linking career interests to global university pathways.
- International university search: Filters by country, course, language and entry criteria, including SAT/ACT and IELTS requirements.
- Common App integration: Allows teachers to upload references and transcripts directly to US universities.
- Skills tracking: Helps students reflect on activities and competencies for use in essays and interviews.
- Shortlisting tools: Enable students to build and compare longlists, then narrow these into final applications with adviser oversight.
- Insights and analytics: Helps schools track trends and outcomes across international applications.

While Unifrog covers a wide range of destinations, some countries are not comprehensively listed, and entry requirements need to be verified against official sources.

BridgeU

BridgeU is another international guidance platform used in many global and IB schools. Its features include:

- University matching algorithm: Matches students to courses based on academic fit, aspirations and location preferences.

- Document centre: Centralises application materials and teacher references.
- Essay tools: Offers writing support and prompts for US and Canadian applications.
- Insights and analytics: Helps schools track trends and outcomes across international applications.

Curriculum planning and guidance delivery

Both platforms can be used to structure a spiralling guidance curriculum throughout secondary school. Activities, research tasks and reflections can be integrated into Personal, Social, Health and Economic Education (PSHE), tutor time or careers lessons. Advisers can set deadlines, monitor progress and document guidance in one place.

Other tools and practices

For schools without access to a dedicated platform, Google Classroom or shared drives can be effective for managing document collection, distributing deadlines and communicating with students and families. Simple shared spreadsheets and forms can track references, personal statements and application progress.

Match: Powered by Concourse

For schools seeking a more proactive approach to university admissions, Match offers an innovative solution. Rather than requiring students to apply, the platform enables universities to make direct admissions and scholarship offers based on anonymised student profiles.

This reverse admissions model reduces stress, removes application barriers and often results in students receiving offers from institutions they might not have otherwise considered. The service is free for students, advisers and schools; participating universities pay a fee to access the platform and engage with prospective students.

Match promotes greater access and equity in higher education as the student or their parents do not pay to use it. According to EAB, over 325,000 offers and £11 billion (~ $14 billion) in scholarships have been extended through Match since its launch, many to students who would not have applied traditionally (EAB, 2023), a considerable additional benefit. In practice, Match can also be useful for students with lower predicted grades or non-standard qualifications, because it spreads the net wide and removes the need for multiple applications from a student who may already be struggling academically.

Meto: Expanding global reach

Meto follows a similar reverse admissions model, with a strong focus on international access. Students create a free profile, which universities use to search for and contact potential applicants – no applications required.

The service is free for students, advisers and schools; universities pay to engage. Meto is particularly valuable for students in underrepresented regions, helping them connect with institutions they may not have otherwise considered.

Counselling practice and standards

As international university guidance becomes more complex, the need for clear, consistent and professional counselling practices has never been greater. Advisers must balance multiple application systems, varied documentation requirements and the pastoral needs of students and families. Establishing strong standards, clear processes and effective communication tools can make international guidance more manageable and more impactful.

A note on private educational agents

Engaging a private educational agent is not necessary for a successful university application. Most students navigate the process effectively with support from their school or college, alongside official university guidance.

Nevertheless, some families – particularly those applying to several countries, or with greater financial flexibility – may choose to work with an agent. Costs can vary significantly. Some agents are paid directly by the family, either through fixed packages or hourly rates, while others receive commission from universities. High-end, multi-destination services can cost up to £14,000.

Where agents are involved, it is important to understand the basis on which they operate. Commission-based arrangements, in particular, may compromise impartiality, especially where advice appears skewed towards certain institutions or overly focused on rankings.

In such cases, it is advisable to hold an early meeting involving the agent, family and the school. This helps clarify roles, set expectations and ensure the student's interests remain the priority throughout the process.

Ultimately, the aim should be to identify the most suitable course and environment for each student. Long-term success and fulfilment are more likely when choices reflect a good personal and academic fit, rather than being driven solely by institutional prestige.

Understanding application routes:
Direct v. portal-based systems

University application systems vary not only from country to country, but sometimes even between institutions within the same country. In some destinations – such as the UK (via UCAS), the Netherlands (via Studielink) and the US (via Common App) – a centralised platform is used to apply to multiple universities. These systems typically offer consistent formats, shared deadlines and easier document coordination.

Elsewhere, including in Spain, Italy and parts of Germany, students apply directly to individual universities. In some countries, both options exist. For example, Australian institutions often operate dual routes: local applicants typically use state-based portals (such as UAC in New South Wales), while international students are directed to apply directly to the university. Some universities in Europe and Asia also allow students to apply either through a national platform or directly to the institution.

It is important to note that local and international applicants are sometimes required to use different systems, even when applying to the same university – so a knowledge of your student's nationality is essential. Application timelines, entry criteria and required documentation may also differ.

Advisers should always encourage students to check the correct application process before submitting. If information online is unclear or contradictory, a brief, courteous email to the university's admissions team is usually enough to confirm the correct route. This step helps avoid misdirected applications, missed deadlines or incomplete submissions.

Managing references for multi-system applications

Unlike the UK, where a single adviser-written reference is standard, many international systems require multiple contributors. US universities typically request individual recommendations from subject teachers alongside a counsellor letter that contextualises the student's academic profile and personal qualities. Systems in Canada, Singapore and Hong Kong may also expect multiple documents, including transcripts and school profiles.

- Create internal timelines for collecting reference requests early in Year 13.
- Use shared platforms (e.g. Unifrog or Google Forms) to gather teacher input.
- Provide teachers with templates and examples for US-style letters.
- Track submissions centrally to ensure nothing is missed.

Using digital coordination tools

Google Classroom, Microsoft Teams and collaborative drives can provide a shared space for storing application documents, guidance meeting notes and deadlines. These tools help keep communication transparent and accessible for students, teachers and parents.

- Set up folders by country or application type.
- Share document checklists and step-by-step timelines.

Maintaining records and evidence

Effective counselling practice includes keeping detailed records of student meetings, application plans and final destinations. This supports safeguarding, helps track outcomes and provides evidence of impact for school improvement planning.

- Keep confidential notes after each student meeting.
- Log deadlines, application stages and submission confirmations. Encourage students to share this responsibility – the more people checking, the less likely something will be missed.
- Record offers and final enrolments for tracking and reporting.

Applying standards in international contexts

Although most international systems do not have a formal equivalent to the Gatsby Benchmarks, UK-based schools can still map their global guidance provision against these standards. The ISCA (International School Counsellor Association) Student Standards may also be a helpful reference, offering a framework for developing students' career readiness, academic planning and personal growth across cultural contexts.

Handling disagreements between students and parents

Disagreements between students and their parents over which course or career path to pursue are not unusual. Parents may be influenced by long-term stability, earning potential or family expectations, while students are guided by personal interests, values and ambitions. These differences can create tension during what is already a complex and emotional process. A Sutton Trust review noted that families who can provide financial or practical support are also more likely to influence decisions about post-18 options – suggesting this privilege may sometimes lead to disagreements when students want to take alternative paths (Sutton Trust, 2018).

It should be emphasised that it is the responsibility of the adviser to act as an advocate for the student, ensuring that their voice is heard and that their preferences are taken seriously. Advisers should aim to facilitate balanced, respectful conversations, helping both parties to understand each other's viewpoints and the reasoning behind them. Where possible, a joint meeting involving the student, parents or carers and the adviser should be arranged. This provides a neutral setting in which to explore concerns, clarify information and work towards a resolution.

Evidence-based tools such as Morrisby can be especially helpful in these situations. These platforms offer clear, personalised data on a student's strengths, preferences and potential career matches. By grounding the discussion in objective insight, advisers can help move the conversation away from emotion or assumption and towards informed decision-making.

Above all, the focus should remain on the student: their goals, their aptitudes and their right to make a considered and supported choice. A successful outcome is one in which the student feels confident in their decision, ideally with their family's understanding and encouragement.

By developing a structured, evidence-informed approach to international counselling, schools can offer students a more consistent and supportive experience – one that empowers them to explore their global options with clarity and confidence.

Case study: Navigating course selection conflicts — Liz's journey

Liz, a Year 12 student with a passion for English literature, aspired to pursue a degree in the subject, aiming for a future career in journalism. Her father, however, advocated for a degree in Hospitality Management, viewing it as a more vocational and financially secure path. He was initially unwilling to support Liz's choice financially, leading to significant tension and emotional distress for Liz, who sought guidance from her school's careers adviser.

Recognising the importance of addressing the conflict constructively, the adviser arranged a meeting with Liz and her parents to facilitate an open discussion. During the meeting, the adviser presented Liz's Morrisby report, which highlighted her strong aptitude for literacy, critical thinking and communication — key competencies for a successful career in journalism. This evidence-based approach helped Liz's father appreciate her strengths and the alignment of her interests with her chosen field.

To further support the discussion, the adviser provided information on postgraduate journalism programmes in the Netherlands, her preferred country for Higher Education (HE), illustrating a clear academic and career progression. Examples included:

- University of Groningen: Offers an English-taught Master's track in Journalism, combining academic coursework with practical journalism skills over 18 months.
- Erasmus Mundus Journalism Master's Programme: A prestigious joint degree funded by the EU, offering full scholarships that cover tuition fees and provide a monthly living stipend, focusing on global journalism education.

These options demonstrated viable pathways for Liz to achieve her career goals, potentially with financial support through scholarships.

The meeting concluded with a mutual understanding: Liz would pursue her passion for English literature, with the long-term goal of entering journalism, and her father eventually agreed to support her decision, recognising the value of aligning career choices with individual strengths and interests.

Conclusion

International university guidance is no longer a niche offering — it is a growing area of practice that requires curiosity, clarity and confidence from advisers. Whether supporting a single student applying to one overseas course or managing dozens of global applications each year, the adviser's role is to provide structure, encouragement and informed support.

Recent trends underscore the urgency of this work. Students are increasingly looking beyond traditional destinations, with countries such as the Netherlands, Portugal and Canada gaining popularity due to more accessible entry routes and clearer post-study pathways (Economic Times, 2024). At the same time, shifting attitudes towards employment – particularly among Gen Z – have led to a rise in interest in vocational, skills-based and stability-focused careers (Business Insider, 2025).

By understanding the differences between global systems, using the right digital tools and embedding international aspirations into long-term planning, advisers can help students access exciting opportunities around the world. Just as importantly, they can foster a sense of independence, global awareness and ambition that stays with students far beyond the application process.

As the later chapters explore regional case studies and institutional insights, advisers will see how these principles play out in practice – helping you to deepen students' knowledge and grow your confidence in delivering truly global guidance.

Adviser checklist

Early planning
- [x] Introduce global HE options from Year 9.
- [x] Guide subject choices to keep pathways open.
- [x] Promote language learning and enrichment activities.
- [x] Encourage early research into systems and destinations.

Profile development
- [x] Use platforms (e.g. Unifrog, BridgeU or shared Google Sheets) to track progress.
- [x] Support CV building and skills reflection.
- [x] Plan for required testing by Year 11.
- [x] Recommend MOOCs, summer schools or leadership roles.

Application support
- [x] Publish timelines across application systems.
- [x] Coordinate references early with templates and examples.
- [x] Provide essay feedback and shortlist advice.
- [x] Centralise documents and track submissions.

Working with families
- [x] Hold regular check-ins with students and parents.
- [x] Facilitate meetings in case of disagreement.
- [x] Use tools (e.g. Morrisby) to inform decisions.
- [x] Prioritise student voice and wellbeing.

Education agents
- [x] Clarify that agents are not necessary.
- [x] Advise on costs and limitations.
- [x] Meet early to define roles if engaged.

2 University guidance in a global context

- ☑ Retain school control of references and transcripts.
- ☑ Keep a brief record of interactions.

Professional practice
- ☑ Align guidance with Gatsby or ISCA standards.
- ☑ Support staff with reference writing.
- ☑ Track outcomes and maintain clear records.

FURTHER INFORMATION

International ACAC (International Association for College Admission Counseling): A global membership organisation that supports and connects professionals involved in international university admissions and school counselling, with a focus on ethical practice, collaboration and student access.
https://www.internationalacac.org/

International School Counsellor Association (ISCA): Offers counselling standards, training materials and professional development opportunities tailored to international school settings.
www.iscainfo.com

Fulbright Commission (UK): Provides information and support for advisers and students interested in US study, including scholarships, webinars and events.
www.fulbright.org.uk

Council of International Schools (CIS): Global network offering guidance standards, university admission forums and school accreditation with a focus on internationalism and ethics.
www.cois.org

British Council: Insights into global education trends, international qualifications and UK recognition abroad.
www.britishcouncil.org

The PIE News: A leading source of news, analysis and commentary on international education, useful for staying updated on policy and admissions developments.
www.thepienews.com

Careers Development Institute (CDI): UK-based guidance frameworks that can inform globally relevant counselling practice.
www.thecdi.net

Gatsby Benchmarks: A framework for high-quality careers guidance. Benchmarks 3, 7 and 8 are particularly relevant when developing international pathways.
www.goodcareerguidance.org.uk

Match: Powered by Concourse – https://discover.concourseglobal.net/student/start

Meto – https://meto-intl.org

3 Guiding the way: Decoding subject choices and careers

> **This chapter will:**
> - Help advisers support students in Years 8 to 11 as they navigate subject choices that influence future academic and career opportunities.
> - Clarify the difference between required and preferred subjects for university courses, dispelling common misconceptions that could limit progression.
> - Highlight how digital tools like Morrisby, BridgeU and Unifrog can guide decision-making through aptitude assessments and global university comparisons.
> - Emphasise the importance of open, student-led discussions that balance ambition with realistic expectations, safeguarding motivation and wellbeing.
> - Reinforce the value of choosing subjects that build transferable skills and flexibility, preparing students for success in an evolving global workplace.

Introduction

Choosing the right school subjects is one of the first significant decisions young people make, and it's a choice that can have a big impact on their career. For advisers of students in Years 8 to 11, it is essential to understand how to support these decisions effectively.

This chapter offers guidance for engaging in meaningful conversations with your students about their interests, strengths and aspirations. It also explores useful tools that can assist in the decision-making process, including Morrisby, BridgeU and Unifrog. You can ensure your charges keep as many doors open as possible if they're armed with a deeper understanding of subject combinations, career planning and long-term academic goals.

Case study: A pathway to Medicine in Australia

Sophie, a Year 11 student attending a school in the North of the UK, has her sights set on studying Medicine. From a young age, she has shown a deep interest in the sciences, particularly human biology, and has shown strong analytical skills and compassion – key traits for a future doctor.

Sophie's subject choices reflect the academic expectations for undergraduate Medicine. She will take mathematics, chemistry and biology at A level, which are highly recommended by medical schools. Sophie is considering an international experience for her higher education. Australia has been proposed by her family as she has an uncle living there, who could provide emotional support and potentially some accommodation. Universities, such as Sydney and Monash, expect a strong background in chemistry and mathematics, while biology is often preferred. Sophie chose mathematics not only because it is required but also because it supports the quantitative aspects of her science studies and future university assessments.

In addition to her academic work, Sophie has volunteered regularly at a local care home and completed shadowing placements at a clinic and hospital. These experiences helped her confirm her commitment to a medical career and will strengthen her application to universities, where admissions increasingly take into account personal qualities and community involvement.

Using platforms like BridgeU and Unifrog, Sophie compared the medical programmes offered in different states of Australia to the UK and built a shortlist based on course structure, entry requirements and lifestyle fit. She and her family also consulted with her school's careers adviser to map out application timelines, ensuring she could meet the deadlines for each university's admission cycle, which differs from the UCAS process. Together, they also drew up a table listing the advantages and disadvantages of Australia versus the UK – always useful when the student has a difficult dilemma. In the end, she decided to make a direct application to the University of Sydney, as the course length is comparable to UK medical schools (5–6 years). For Sophie, it was a lifestyle decision, coupled with her family connections.

Sophie is now preparing for the UCAT ANZ (University Clinical Aptitude Test for Australia and New Zealand), an essential admissions test used by many Australian medical schools. She is also aware that some universities may require an interview as part of their selection process, so she has joined her school's debating club to refine her public speaking and critical thinking skills.

Sophie's profile exemplifies a well-rounded applicant: strong academic performance in relevant subjects, meaningful and directly linked extracurricular activities, early engagement with university entry tests and a clear understanding of the international application process. She is likely to receive an offer.

3 Guiding the way: decoding subject choices and careers

> **Decision point**
>
> Sophie had to choose between staying in the UK for Medicine or applying to Australian universities, weighing family ties, course structure and long-term lifestyle fit.
>
> **Adviser insight**
>
> Advisers can help students compare international options by breaking down admissions tests, timelines and application formats. Encourage students to list pros and cons early on so decisions are rooted in evidence, not assumptions.

The importance of subject choices

Navigating subject and career choices is a pivotal aspect of a child's academic and professional journey. For advisers and teachers of children in Year 8 to 11, these years represent a crucial period for shaping future aspirations. The subjects chosen at GCSE and subsequently at A level or IB can dictate the pathways available for higher education and future careers. Some subjects are prerequisites for specific university courses, while others can help to keep a broad range of options open.

For students aspiring to enter Medicine, a strong foundation in chemistry and mathematics is essential, with biology perhaps surprisingly often only recommended (as medical schools argue that the biology content is taught). Law does not require specific subjects, but history and English can help develop critical thinking and analytical skills.

Engineering requires a solid background in mathematics and physics, with some courses also requiring chemistry. Dentistry typically requires mathematics and chemistry, with biology or physics being advantageous. Pharmacy and Veterinary Science share similar requirements. Finance, Economics, Architecture and Computer Science all have particular subject expectations, with mathematics often being central.

Choosing subjects with care ensures that students can pursue their desired career pathways while keeping options open for unforeseen changes in interests or goals.

A typical curriculum model throughout the world

Figure 3.1 (overleaf) shows a typical curriculum model followed by UK and international schools throughout the world. GCE Advanced Level (A level) remains the gold standard for admission to universities internationally within the UK curriculum. The International Baccalaureate (IB) is an alternative qualification favoured by some private UK schools and many international schools for its broader curriculum and compulsory engagement with the community. For a few careers, such as Medicine and Engineering, you would expect to see mathematics taken right to the top of the pyramid to ensure no potential pathways are removed.

FIGURE 3.1 A typical curriculum model.

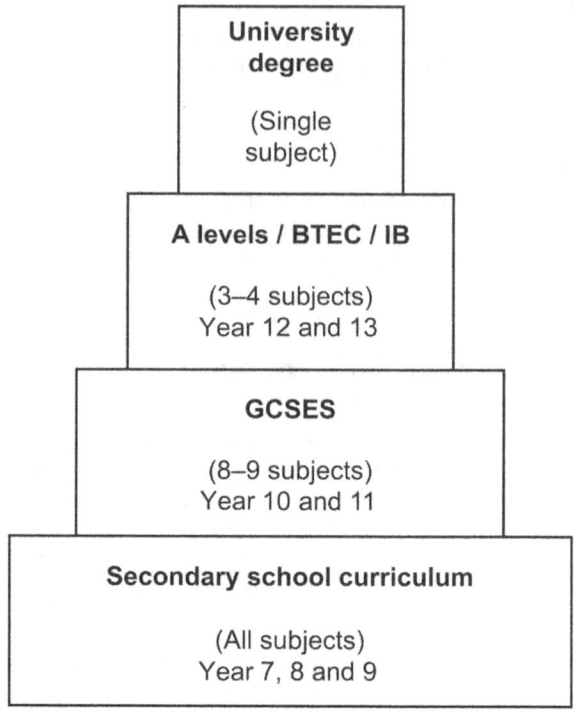

Compulsory and core subjects: How demanding are they?

Most schools require students to take compulsory subjects such as mathematics, English and science at GCSE (or IGCSE, which is widely accepted as equivalent by universities globally and can be used interchangeably for guidance purposes). Beyond these, students can usually choose additional subjects based on their interests and aspirations. Subjects become more challenging at each level. A subject that may seem interesting or manageable in Year 9 will become more demanding at GCSE and even more so at A level. Students must be prepared for this increase in difficulty and understand what the subject entails in terms of content, assessment and workload.

Subject combinations: Key considerations

Several key factors should be considered when selecting subject combinations:

1. Career goals.
2. Ability.
3. Interest and enjoyment.

First, advisers, students, and their families should reflect on future plans: What does the student want to do after school? If a clear career goal exists, it's essential to research the subject requirements for that field. If students are still undecided, it is wise to choose a broad and balanced combination that will allow flexibility later on.

Students should think about which subjects they enjoy and excel in. Success often correlates strongly with interest and aptitude. Ambition is important, but it must be balanced with realistic expectations. Problems often emerge when parents attempt to live their lives through their children – a relatively common occurrence. In extreme circumstances, it can lead to rifts in families that take years to settle. Teacher and adviser feedback is invaluable here, offering insight into whether a student is likely to thrive in a particular subject and subsequent career.

Students may also be interested in exploring new subjects not previously studied – such as psychology, economics or computer science. These can open up new career pathways but should be chosen only after careful research into what the subject involves. It is important to understand not only the topics covered, but also the method of assessment, whether through coursework, written exams or practical work.

Dispelling the myths around subject requirements

Many misconceptions surround which subjects are required for certain degrees. For example, although chemistry is mandatory for Medicine, biology may not be required by every university. Engineering typically requires mathematics and physics, but chemistry is not always essential unless the course is in Chemical Engineering. In Architecture, while art can be beneficial, some universities place greater emphasis on the student's portfolio rather than specific subject choices.

Advisers, when supporting their students, should check university admissions criteria carefully and research using reliable guidance platforms to avoid limiting options based on misunderstandings. Many universities also list certain A level subjects as 'preferred' rather than 'required'. This distinction is important: while a subject may not be mandatory for entry into a particular course, having it can significantly strengthen an application or provide useful preparation for the content of the degree.

For example, while economics is rarely a required A level subject for an Economics degree, mathematics is often essential, and more competitive institutions prefer further mathematics. Similarly, English literature is frequently viewed favourably by admissions tutors for its analytical and essay-writing focus. Understanding the difference between required and preferred subjects allows students to make strategic choices that enhance their prospects without unnecessarily restricting their subject combinations.

The impact of dropping subjects

Dropping certain subjects after GCSE may make it difficult to pick them up again at A level or university level. For instance, dropping mathematics could limit opportunities in fields like economics or engineering. If a student decides to discontinue a subject, it should be a well-considered decision that takes long-term goals into account.

Don't panic: Focus on the bigger picture

While subject choices matter, they are not the sole determinants of future success. A calm, thoughtful approach to decision-making is best. Encouraging your charge to make informed choices based on their interests, abilities and goals will yield the best results in the long run.

Keeping options open

Choosing 'facilitating' subjects – such as mathematics, English, the sciences, history, geography and languages – can help students maintain flexibility for a wide range of future opportunities. These subjects are valued by many universities and employers and equip students with transferable skills like problem-solving, analysis and communication.

The importance of mathematics in particular has become increasingly significant in recent years, not only for science-based degrees but also for courses in economics, business, psychology, social sciences and even the arts. Strong mathematical skills demonstrate logical thinking and adaptability, and they open doors to a broad spectrum of careers. Employers in fields as diverse as technology, finance, healthcare and media look for graduates who can interpret data, work with numbers confidently and apply quantitative reasoning to real-world challenges.

A student who is unsure about their future career should combine subjects that keep as many doors open as possible, rather than narrowing their path too early. It is easier to specialise later than to reintroduce a subject that has been dropped.

Useful tools for guidance: Morrisby, BridgeU and Unifrog

Several platforms offer structured support based on aptitude, interests and academic goals to assist students and parents in making informed decisions. These include Morrisby, BridgeU and Unifrog – the last two having been discussed in detail in the previous chapter.

Morrisby

The Morrisby Profile is a psychometric assessment designed to help individuals make career and educational choices based on natural aptitudes and preferences. It includes assessments in verbal, numerical, spatial, abstract and mechanical reasoning. Results are not based on learned knowledge, making the tool useful for identifying latent strengths. Morrisby (a UK-based company, but may be used globally) also includes career interest questionnaires that provide insights into different work environments, styles and preferences.

These assessments generate personalised suggestions for subject choices and career paths. Schools often use it; it costs approximately £25 to £75 depending on the package. The tool can help advisers, particularly when there is a mismatch between what the parents would like the student to pursue and the student's preference. The results can provide the adviser with useful information when advocating for the student. It also provides a valuable starting point for a student who is entirely unclear about their future career pathway.

BridgeU

BridgeU supports students with global university and career planning. It includes a university matching tool, career exploration resources and support with personal statements and applications. It is particularly helpful for students applying internationally, offering guidance on entry requirements, admissions processes and course comparisons across multiple countries.

Unifrog

Unifrog is widely used in the UK and by international schools. It offers an intuitive and comprehensive careers library, apprenticeship and university search tools, and resources for skill development. Students can compare university courses, look at job profiles and explore new subject areas. Unifrog also supports CV building and interview preparation. It is particularly strong at levelling the playing field, ensuring that all students have access to accurate, up-to-date information regardless of background.

Fostering meaningful discussions

Advisers play a crucial role in supporting students through these decisions. Open and constructive conversations can help children articulate their goals and address concerns. Asking open-ended questions such as, 'What subjects or activities do you find most engaging and why?' can help students reflect more deeply. Encouraging exploration through extracurricular activities, internships or shadowing opportunities can also offer valuable insight.

Pressuring students into taking subjects they are not interested in comes with a risk. While guidance is crucial, autonomy in the decision-making process builds confidence and responsibility. A student is more likely to achieve strong outcomes and stay motivated throughout their course if they study what they enjoy and are good at.

International applications and global considerations

For families considering higher education beyond the UK, it is vital to understand how subject choices align with international university systems. In countries such as the US and Canada, students are often admitted to universities based on overall academic achievement rather than specific subject combinations. This allows for more flexibility and experimentation.

However, students will still need to demonstrate academic rigour, critical thinking and subject depth through A levels or equivalent qualifications for selective courses or institutions. These include Ivy League schools or Canadian medical programmes. Most US universities admit using SAT results (for which there is no exemption for UK or international students), but A level provides an excellent complement to these.

In European countries, including Germany and the Netherlands, certain courses may have direct subject prerequisites for admission, particularly for Science or Engineering. In Australia and New Zealand, universities often require English and mathematics as part of their entrance criteria, along with prerequisites for specialised fields. In Asia, particularly Singapore and Hong Kong, competitive institutions may have expectations similar to those in the UK, placing value on subject relevance and academic achievement.

Students applying internationally should consult the admissions websites of their target universities or work with a careers adviser who understands global application routes. Platforms like BridgeU and Unifrog are particularly helpful in comparing international requirements and supporting the application process across multiple countries.

Careers advice for specific subjects

Medicine-related careers

Some careers have particularly well-defined routes from subject choice to university study and beyond. For example, as already mentioned, Medicine remains one of the most structured pathways. Dentistry, Pharmacy and Veterinary Science share similar high academic expectations, and competition for places can be very intense.

Students considering these routes should demonstrate strong performance across science and maths, ideally supported by relevant work experience or internships in a relevant working context. Having said that, there are a few medical schools globally that specialise in accepting students into Medicine and related courses with lower grades, but the participants pay the price in higher fees.

Engineering

Engineering obviously requires a robust foundation in mathematics and physics, and in some cases, chemistry. Students applying for courses such as Civil, Mechanical, Electrical or Aerospace Engineering will be expected to show high-level problem-solving and analytical thinking skills, with many universities introducing compulsory admissions tests to assess these.

Computer Science

For Computer Science, mathematics is non-negotiable, and many universities prefer or require further mathematics as well. A strong programming portfolio or relevant project work can also strengthen an application.

Law and Politics

Law, while having no mandatory A level subjects, benefits from rigorous essay-based subjects such as history or English literature. These help students develop skills in critical reading, writing and argumentation. Similarly, degrees in Politics, International Relations (IR) or Philosophy benefit from subjects that promote deep thinking and analytical reasoning.

Creative industries

Creative industries often require a different kind of preparation. Architecture may require art, but more importantly, a well-developed portfolio. Students interested in Design, Fashion or Film should prioritise subjects that allow them to build a body of work, such as art and design or media studies. Music degrees often require formal study of Music and additional qualifications, such as the Royal School of Music ABRSM grades.

Finance

In Finance, Economics and Accounting, mathematics is central. Economics A level, while not always required, is often desirable. For highly selective courses, further mathematics can enhance a student's profile. Business degrees, on the other hand, are accessible through a wide range of subject backgrounds, though Business Studies and Economics can offer a helpful foundation which will make the workload more manageable at undergraduate level.

Case study: Studying Architecture in the Netherlands

Louca is a Year 12 student who has always been fascinated by buildings and design. From a young age, he enjoyed sketching, building models and thinking about how environments shape the way people live and interact. Now, he is considering an application to the Eindhoven University of Technology (TU/e) in the Netherlands to study Architecture, Urbanism and Building Sciences.

Studying in the Netherlands appeals to Louca because of its practical, project-based approach and international student community. In consultation with the head of sixth form at his school, he discovered the tuition fees are comparatively affordable compared to the US or UK, and the teaching style promotes independence – something he values highly.

Louca's A level choices include mathematics, physics, and art and design – a well-rounded combination that demonstrates his ability in technical, analytical and creative fields. These subjects not only align with entry expectations for Architecture programmes in the UK and the Netherlands but also prepare him for the problem-solving and spatial reasoning required in the degree.

A strong portfolio is essential for most architecture-related degrees, although Eindhoven University of Technology (TU/e) does not require art at A level. Louca has spent time carefully curating a collection of both school and personal projects.

He has also participated in extracurricular activities including a design club and completed an online course in sustainable architecture. His interest in environmental issues aligns with the Eindhoven University of Technology's emphasis on innovation and sustainable urban development.

Louca is now preparing his application through Studielink, the centralised Dutch university application system. He is aware that Dutch universities often teach in English at the undergraduate level (but may require evidence of English proficiency such as IELTS, if English is not the student's first language). He has also been researching the Dutch higher education system through BridgeU, where he found detailed information on course structure, university rankings and student life in the Netherlands. For Louca, his decision was swayed by the good value on fees and the international experience. He is on track to pursue his passion for Architecture in a global context through careful planning, strong academic preparation and a compelling portfolio.

Decision point

Louca's choice involved balancing subject requirements for Architecture with his preference for an international learning environment that supported independence and sustainability.

Adviser insight

For creative courses, advisers can reinforce the importance of portfolios and encourage students to seek feedback on their work. Understanding regional differences in entry expectations (e.g. portfolio v. specific subjects) is key.

Portable skills for the future

Beyond subject knowledge, today's workplace demands a wide range of transferable skills. These include communication, collaboration, digital literacy, resilience, critical thinking and creativity. Many of these skills are not tied to a specific subject but are developed through learning itself – especially when students challenge themselves with a varied and balanced subject combination.

For instance, a student studying history will hone their ability to analyse information, evaluate sources and construct persuasive arguments. A Language student will strengthen communication and memory, while someone studying mathematics will develop precision and logical thinking. Teamwork and presentation skills often come through practical projects in subjects like science or design technology.

Employers are placing growing value on adaptability given increasing automation (often through AI) and the rapid change in the job market. Students who can think critically, work independently and collaboratively, and communicate clearly will be better equipped to thrive in diverse careers. Subject choices that nurture these abilities are investments in a student's lifelong employability.

Degree requirements at a glance

Table 3.1 summarises commonly chosen university degree courses, alongside subjects that universities typically require and those that are preferred or advantageous. Please use this guidance alongside specific university entry requirements, which can vary by institution.

TABLE 3.1 Degree requirements

Degree course	Required subjects	Preferred subjects
Medicine	Chemistry, biology, mathematics (varies)	Physics
Dentistry	Chemistry, biology, mathematics (varies)	Physics
Pharmacy	Chemistry, biology, mathematics (varies)	Physics
Veterinary Science	Chemistry, biology, mathematics (varies)	Physics
Engineering	Mathematics, physics	Further mathematics, chemistry
Computer Science	Mathematics	Further mathematics, physics
Architecture	Usually art (varies)	Mathematics, design and technology, physics
Law	None	History, English literature, politics
Economics	Mathematics	Further mathematics, economics
Finance	Mathematics	Further mathematics, economics
Accounting	Mathematics	Business studies, economics
Psychology	Sometimes biology	Mathematics, English literature
Politics/IR	None	History, politics, economics
English Literature	English literature	History, drama
History	History	English literature, politics
Business Management	None	Business studies, economics
Sociology/Anthropology	None	Sociology, geography
Media and Communications	None	English literature, media studies
Art and Design	Art or design-based subject	Photography, media studies

Note: Subjects required for medicine
Entry requirements for Medicine vary significantly between countries, so it's important to choose A level subjects with flexibility in mind. Chemistry is almost always required, making it a non-negotiable choice for most applicants. Biology is either required or strongly preferred in many systems (including the UK). Mathematics is often expected in countries such as Australia and is generally recommended as a third subject. Physics may sometimes be accepted as a substitute for one of the core sciences, but it is rarely required in its own right. Students considering international applications should always check the subject expectations for each university carefully.

Final thoughts

Choosing subjects for GCSE and A level is a significant milestone, but it need not be a stressful one. There's no doubt students can make informed decisions that set them on a path towards academic and professional success. But they need access to high-quality information, input from teachers and career advisers and thoughtful conversations at home. Subject choices are not about locking in a career at age 14, but about laying strong foundations. Students can make confident, flexible choices by prioritising interests, strengths and long-term goals. Platforms like Morrisby, BridgeU and Unifrog provide added insight and reassurance, helping students make evidence-based decisions that reflect both who they are and who they want to become.

Adviser checklist

Start early - Ideally by Year 8 or 9
- [x] Encourage students to explore strengths, interests and future goals.
- [x] Begin conversations about how subject choices link to possible careers.
- [x] Promote awareness of the increasing difficulty of subjects at higher levels.

Use evidence-based tools
- [x] Introduce platforms like Morrisby, BridgeU and Unifrog to support career matching and subject selection.
- [x] Help students and parents interpret aptitude profiles and subject recommendations.
- [x] Use digital comparisons to explore global university entry requirements.

Clarify entry requirements
- [x] Distinguish between required and preferred subjects for common degree courses.
- [x] Use current university guidance to challenge myths and prevent limiting choices.
- [x] Emphasise the risks of dropping core subjects like mathematics or sciences too early.

Promote flexibility
- [x] Encourage a broad and balanced subject combination, especially for undecided students.
- [x] Highlight the value of 'facilitating' subjects for keeping options open.
- [x] Support decision-making that balances ambition with ability and wellbeing.

Facilitate informed conversations
- [x] Guide students to reflect on enjoyment, performance and long-term plans.
- [x] Navigate parent–student disagreements with care and objectivity.
- [x] Encourage realistic expectations and manage the emotional aspects of choice.

Consider global aspirations

- ☑ Advise students considering international universities on how subject choices align with different systems and explain how requirements vary across countries and courses.
- ☑ Encourage use of tools like BridgeU to map international pathways.

Support portfolios and preparation

- ☑ For creative subjects, ensure students understand portfolio requirements and deadlines.
- ☑ Suggest extracurricular activities, projects or online courses to enhance applications.
- ☑ Reinforce the importance of strong written and verbal communication for essay-based subjects.

Reinforce transferable skills

- ☑ Emphasise how subjects develop core skills: analysis, communication, critical thinking and collaboration.
- ☑ Show how these skills apply across multiple career sectors.

Stay involved

- ☑ Revisit subject and career discussions regularly – especially at GCSE and post-16 transition points.
- ☑ Work with teachers and parents to ensure advice is joined-up and student-centred.

FURTHER INFORMATION

For additional resources and guidance, visit the official websites of the organisations mentioned:

Morrisby – https://www.morrisby.com

BridgeU – https://www.bridge-u.com

Unifrog – https://www.unifrog.org

4 Making your application stand out

This chapter will:

- Explain how international university systems assess students beyond academic grades, and the adviser's role in supporting effective self-presentation.
- Provide guidance on writing personal essays for the US, letters of motivation for Europe and statements for portfolio-based creative courses.
- Explore how extracurricular and super curricular activities can enhance applications, and how advisers can help students reflect on these meaningfully.
- Recommend enrichment tools such as MOOCs, lectures and competitions to support academic curiosity and subject alignment.
- Address the ethical use of AI in application writing, offering practical advice on maintaining authenticity.

The adviser's role in a global application landscape

In an increasingly competitive and globalised higher education market, students applying to international universities face the challenge of distinguishing themselves in a crowded field. For advisers, this presents both an opportunity and a responsibility: to guide students in presenting themselves with clarity, depth and integrity across a range of application formats and cultural expectations.

While strong academic performance remains a critical factor, most international systems look beyond grades when evaluating applicants. From personal essays in the US to letters of motivation in Europe and portfolio submissions in creative disciplines, institutions are asking students to demonstrate who they are, not just what they know. The quality of this self-presentation often reflects the quality of the advising that supports it.

This chapter focuses on the key components of standout international applications, with practical guidance on how advisers can support students in developing compelling narratives, identifying meaningful experiences and aligning their interests with institutional offerings. It offers strategies for advising on reflective writing, enriching academic profiles and using tools such as MOOCs and internships to build credible, authentic applications. It also tackles the increasingly important topic of artificial intelligence – how students are using it, and how advisers can help ensure its ethical use in the application process.

Advisers occupy a pivotal position in this landscape. Whether working with students one-on-one or delivering guidance through workshops and group sessions, they have the chance to shape not only the quality of applications, but the confidence with which students express their aspirations. A well-supported applicant is more likely to present a clear sense of purpose – and it is often this clarity that sets them apart.

Guiding students through the US college essay

For students applying to universities in the US, the college essay is often the most distinctive and personal part of the application. Unlike systems where academic achievement alone is the principal focus, US admissions place considerable emphasis on a student's capacity for reflection, originality and self-awareness. The main essay – typically submitted via the Common App – is a chance for applicants to move beyond lists of grades and activities and instead communicate something of who they are, how they think and what they value.

Advisers play a crucial role in helping students approach this task with purpose and authenticity. The most effective essays often stem from small, specific experiences that reveal larger personal insights – not grand achievements, but moments of growth, curiosity or change. Advisers can support students by encouraging them to explore stories that feel honest and meaningful, even if they seem ordinary at first glance.

It is important to emphasise that this essay is not an academic statement, nor is it a persuasive argument in the traditional sense. Instead, it is a reflective narrative. Students should aim to show, not tell – using detail, structure and tone to allow their voice to come through naturally.

Advising strategies include:

- Brainstorming through questioning: Instead of asking students what they want to write about, ask what experiences have challenged them, what they've learnt outside the classroom, or when they've changed their mind about something important.
- Encouraging specificity: General statements such as 'I've always loved helping people' become more powerful when grounded in particular anecdotes, interactions or turning points.
- Avoiding over-editing: While clarity and grammar matter, the student's voice should remain intact. Overly polished or adult-sounding essays often lose the warmth and immediacy that admissions officers are seeking.
- Maintaining boundaries: Some students may feel pressure to disclose trauma or hardship to 'stand out'. Advisers should help students assess whether these stories serve their narrative and whether they are being shared with the right intent and emotional readiness.

In addition to the main essay, many universities require supplementary essays. These are often shorter but demand more precision. Common prompts include 'Why this college?', 'Describe a community you belong to', or 'What academic area excites you and why?' Strong responses demonstrate that the student has researched the institution, understands its offerings and can articulate why it suits their goals.

Encourage students to:

- Refer to specific modules, programmes or campus initiatives.
- Connect personal interests with what the university offers.
- Avoid generic praise – admissions teams can spot copy-and-paste answers easily.

As the volume of international applications to US universities grows, institutions are increasingly alert to recycled essays and AI-generated content. Advisers should reassure students that the goal is not perfection but personality – a well-written piece that reflects thoughtful engagement and a genuine desire to learn.

Case study: What makes a compelling personal essay for the US?

This case study explores how a student used the Common App prompt 'Reflect on a time when you questioned or challenged a belief or idea' to apply for the BA in Public Policy at the University of Michigan. It shows how thoughtful reflection, combined with academic engagement like Model UN, can make a personal essay stand out. A comparison between a strong and weak version highlights what works – and what doesn't.

Example A: Strong extract

In our school's Model United Nations, I signed up to defend a resolution prioritising economic growth over environmental regulation. It wasn't a position I fully supported, but I was curious: Could I understand and articulate the opposing side well enough to challenge my own assumptions?

Preparing for the debate, I leaned into arguments about GDP, employment and industrial competitiveness. But the more I researched, the more I struggled. I'd recently completed a community report on air quality through a local environmental youth group, and I couldn't ignore what I'd seen: real consequences, disproportionately affecting marginalised communities. During the session, I delivered my position – but found myself publicly questioning it by the end.

This experience sparked my deeper interest in public policy. It taught me that intellectual courage isn't about certainty, but about being willing to reconsider. I later led a school-wide discussion on environmental justice and co-authored a policy brief for our city council's youth advisory board.

I'm now applying to the BA in Public Policy at the University of Michigan because of its emphasis on ethical governance and interdisciplinary analysis. The Ford School's focus on equity, combined with opportunities like the Policy Pitch Competition and the course 'Values & Ethics in Public Policy', aligns with my commitment to questioning, reframing and ultimately, creating better solutions.

Why it works:

- Opens with a concrete academic context (Model UN) and a deliberate challenge to the student's views.

- Demonstrates intellectual maturity through research and community involvement.
- Shows a clear shift in perspective backed by action and reflection.
- Names specific course content and values at the University of Michigan.
- Ends with a well-articulated purpose rooted in the student's growth and academic interests.
- Balanced tone: curious, thoughtful and self-aware.

Example B: Weak extract

I've always believed in treating everyone fairly. One time I disagreed with someone who said police officers shouldn't be questioned. I said that wasn't right, because everyone should be held accountable. We argued about it for a while and eventually decided to drop the conversation. I still think I was right, but I also realised that people don't always change their minds, no matter what you say.

After that, I started thinking more about how people form their opinions. I read a few articles online and tried to understand both sides. I didn't come to a final conclusion, but I think it's important to respect people's views. This made me want to study Public Policy so I can work on issues that affect people's lives. I hope to help communities and make fairer laws that everyone can agree on.

Why it falls short:

- Offers a vague and undeveloped narrative without a clear moment of change.
- Lacks detail about the situation or its relevance to the course.
- Fails to connect experience to academic motivation or personal growth.
- No reference to the university, its course content or structure.
- Relies on generalisations rather than insight.

Advising tip

Encourage students to:

- Choose a specific moment that led to questioning or change.
- Show how that moment shaped their values, goals or academic interests.
- Reflect honestly on complexity – growth often starts with uncertainty.
- Ground their narrative in evidence, not platitudes.
- Tie the experience directly to the course and institution they are applying to.

Helping students write letters of motivation for Europe

In contrast to the personal, story-driven essays required by US universities, many European institutions ask applicants to submit a letter of motivation – a concise, formal document that outlines a student's academic interests, reasons for applying and long-term goals. While less reflective than the American essay, this type of writing still offers students the chance to present a focused, purposeful case for admission. For advisers, the challenge is to help students strike the right tone:

clear, professional and goal-oriented, without sounding mechanical or overly generic.

These letters are particularly common in applications to universities in the Netherlands, Germany, France and parts of Scandinavia. Though requirements vary slightly between institutions, the key elements remain consistent. A strong letter will:

- Demonstrate a clear understanding of the programme and what it offers.
- Show alignment between the student's goals and the course structure.
- Explain how the programme supports the student's academic and career trajectory.

Guidance for students applying abroad emphasises that strong motivation letters should clearly demonstrate genuine interest, show an understanding of the chosen programme and link academic interests to the course content. Generic statements or vague enthusiasm are less persuasive than concrete examples of subject engagement or career alignment.

Advisers can support students by encouraging them to begin with concrete motivations. Why this field? Why this course, at this institution? What specific modules, opportunities or teaching styles appeal to them, and why? Rather than writing about their general interest in a subject, students should connect their enthusiasm to their experiences – for example, linking an Extended Project Qualification (EPQ) title or a summer research project to the academic themes of the course.

Letters of motivation should typically be no more than one side of A4, and they should follow a logical structure: an opening paragraph that introduces the student's academic focus, a middle section that discusses programme fit, and a conclusion that outlines future plans. Tone should be formal but sincere – the aim is to sound engaged, not embellished.

Common issues include students struggling to articulate their motivation clearly, failing to reference course content or adopting an inappropriately casual or inflated tone. Advisers should be aware of these patterns and provide structure and feedback to help students avoid them.

Country-specific considerations can be helpful:

- In the Netherlands, many courses are offered in English and value independent thinking; universities often seek students who can articulate clear reasons for choosing a particular programme.
- In Germany, academic rigour and long-term planning are emphasised. Students should show they have researched entry requirements and understand the demands of the course.
- In France, a slightly more personal tone may be acceptable, particularly when referencing cultural interests or language learning, but professionalism remains key.

Advisers should also remind students to proofread carefully and, where relevant, include references to any required academic preparation (e.g. language certificates or subject prerequisites). A strong letter of motivation will not only help secure admission but will also signal a student's readiness for independent university-level study – a key consideration in European systems.

Case study: What makes a strong letter of motivation?

Below are two fuller examples of motivation letter extracts. Each one targets the same course – a BSc Future Planet Studies at the University of Amsterdam – but only one demonstrates the clarity, structure and depth required for a competitive international application. The critique following each sample shows how advisers can help students move from general enthusiasm to specific, persuasive motivation.

Example A: Strong extract

My decision to apply for the BSc in Future Planet Studies at the University of Amsterdam is grounded in a combination of academic exploration and personal commitment. During my IB studies, I developed a strong interest in environmental systems, which I pursued through my Extended Essay on the socio-political impacts of rising sea levels in Southeast Asia. This research sparked my interest in environmental policy as a global issue, and I have since attended virtual lectures by the Grantham Institute and completed the FutureLearn course 'Environmental Challenges: Justice in Natural Resource Management'.

Outside the classroom, I've volunteered with a community rewilding project and helped organise an inter-school sustainability conference. I enjoy applying scientific understanding to real-world contexts and am particularly interested in how environmental science intersects with law, economics and ethics. The University of Amsterdam's interdisciplinary approach, especially the modules in 'Urban Sustainability' and 'Climate Governance', directly aligns with my academic and career goals. I am also drawn to the research-led teaching model and the chance to collaborate with students from diverse backgrounds.

My long-term aim is to work in environmental consultancy or policy development, ideally in a role that allows me to contribute to climate justice initiatives in the Global South. I believe the academic rigour and international perspective offered by your programme provide the ideal foundation for this path.

Why it works:

- Opens with an academic focus and a clear research interest that is later expanded.
- Connects prior learning and extracurricular activities to the course's specific strengths.
- Mentions independent engagement with the subject (extended essay).
- Demonstrates detailed knowledge of the course content and institutional ethos.
- Ends with a clearly stated goal that logically follows from the preceding points.
- Balanced tone: confident, reflective and free from exaggeration.

> **Example B: Weak extract**
>
> I have always loved nature and want to do something to help the planet. I believe studying Future Planet Studies is the right choice for me because I am passionate about saving the environment. During school I studied Biology and Geography, which I enjoyed, especially topics like pollution and ecosystems. I care deeply about the world and want to make a difference.
>
> The University of Amsterdam seems like a great place to study, and I would like to experience life in a new country and meet people from different cultures. I think the course looks interesting and will help me get a good job in the future. I hope to learn a lot and do well in my studies so I can contribute to making the world better.
>
> **Why it falls short:**
>
> - Lacks evidence – no specific experiences, projects or further reading.
> - Uses vague, overused phrases ('make a difference', 'help the planet').
> - References to subject interest are generic and unconvincing.
> - No mention of the course structure, teaching style or specific modules.
> - Prioritises personal lifestyle goals over academic alignment.
> - Ends on a general aspiration with no clearly articulated direction.
>
> **Advising tip**
>
> Encourage students to:
>
> - Anchor their motivation in evidence: coursework, research, reading or personal projects.
> - Name specific modules or features of the programme.
> - Connect experiences to future ambitions with logic and progression.
> - Avoid overstatement – enthusiasm is important, but credibility comes from clarity.

Highlighting extracurricular and super curricular experiences

While academic qualifications remain central to university admissions, many international institutions – particularly in North America, parts of Europe and Asia – place increasing value on what students do beyond the classroom. From leadership roles and volunteering to independent academic exploration, extracurricular and super curricular activities help admissions teams assess a student's motivation, character and broader readiness for university life.

Advisers play a key role in helping students identify these experiences and reflect on them meaningfully. The goal is not to produce a list of achievements, but to highlight growth, skills and personal development. Students often underestimate the value of their involvement, especially if it doesn't carry a formal title or award. Advisers can help draw out quieter examples – a mentoring role, an independent coding project, a family responsibility – and link them to relevant qualities such as initiative, empathy or resilience.

A useful distinction:

- Extracurricular activities include sports, clubs, music, part-time jobs, volunteering or community projects – anything outside the formal curriculum.
- Super curricular activities go beyond what is taught in class but remain academically focused. Examples include attending public lectures, completing online courses, entering essay competitions or reading academic material related to a chosen subject.

Many competitive institutions are looking for evidence of intellectual curiosity – especially in selective courses such as Economics, Law, International Relations or the Sciences. Super curricular exploration shows that a student is willing to learn independently, and can help set them apart from other candidates with similar grades.

Advising strategies include:

- Encouraging students to keep a reflection log of activities, noting what they did, what they learnt and how it shaped their thinking.
- Helping students link experiences to key themes – leadership, collaboration, time management or global awareness.
- Using action-oriented language in written applications, for example, 'organised', 'initiated', 'designed', 'analysed', rather than passive descriptions.

In systems where written components are short – such as supplemental essays or letters of motivation – the integration of these experiences must be concise and relevant. Rather than adding them as a separate paragraph, students should weave them into their narrative to support key claims about their interests or qualities.

For advisers working with younger students (Year 10–11), these conversations can also serve as planning tools: helping students select meaningful opportunities that will feed into their future applications. The emphasis should be on depth over breadth – sustained engagement with a few activities is far more compelling than superficial involvement in many.

Adding depth through MOOCs and academic exploration

One of the most effective ways students can demonstrate genuine academic interest is through independent learning. Increasingly, universities – particularly in the US, Canada and across Europe – value applicants who go beyond the school curriculum to explore their chosen subject in greater depth. For advisers, encouraging and guiding students to engage with this kind of enrichment can make a real difference to the quality and credibility of an international application.

Massive Open Online Courses (MOOCs) are widely accessible and often free. They allow students to study academic content from world-leading institutions (e.g. Harvard) and can help reinforce subject choice, extend knowledge or even spark new interests. Advisers should steer students towards courses that complement their intended area of study, or that offer an interdisciplinary link to broader intellectual themes.

Examples of suitable platforms include:

- FutureLearn (UK and international universities);
- edX (Harvard, MIT, and global partners);
- Coursera (varied academic and practical courses);
- Unifrog (curated subject-specific pathways).

A key point for students – and one that advisers should emphasise – is that the value of a MOOC lies not in its certificate but in its reflection. Students should be prepared to explain *why* they took the course, *what* they learnt and *how* it influenced their thinking or future plans. A sentence in a letter of motivation or college essay that thoughtfully integrates this kind of insight can be more powerful than a list of completions.

Similarly, advisers can encourage students to engage with academic content in other independent ways, such as:

- Reading university-level material or subject-specific journalism.
- Watching academic talks (e.g. TED, Gresham College, Hay Festival lectures).
- Exploring open-access journals or student research forums.
- Participating in academic competitions or discussion groups.

Encouraging students to keep a simple record – what they read or watched, why they chose it and what it made them think about – can be invaluable later in the writing process. This habit of self-directed learning reflects many of the qualities admissions teams seek: curiosity, critical thinking and a willingness to explore complex ideas.

For advisers, recommending targeted resources and helping students frame their learning in a reflective and relevant way is often one of the most practical contributions they can make – especially for students applying to highly selective courses or institutions where subject passion needs to be both evident and credible.

Supporting portfolio-based and creative applications

For students applying to courses in fields such as art, design, architecture, fashion or the performing arts, a portfolio or creative supplement is often a central part of the application. Unlike academic statements or essays, these submissions must demonstrate process, originality and technical skill – all within the framework of each institution's specific requirements. Advisers can play a vital role in helping students navigate these expectations and present their work confidently and coherently.

Portfolio requirements vary considerably across countries and institutions. Some universities may request digital submissions only, while others require an in-person review or interview as part of the selection process. In many cases, students will also be asked to include a written commentary – either as a brief rationale for the work or a reflective statement outlining their creative journey.

Key areas where advisers can support include:

- Clarifying requirements early: Portfolio guidelines can be detailed and specific. Advisers should encourage students to research expectations well in advance, including preferred formats, number of pieces and any contextual documentation required.

- Structuring the submission: A good portfolio tells a story. Students should be guided to select work that shows range and progression – from initial concept to final execution. Where appropriate, process work (e.g. sketchbooks, drafts, experiments) should be included to show how ideas developed over time.
- Focusing on originality: Many institutions are looking for creative risk-taking and an authentic voice rather than technical perfection. Advisers can help students move beyond safe or derivative work and reflect on what inspires them, how they work and what makes their approach distinctive.
- Preparing written elements: When a statement or caption is required, students should be encouraged to write clearly and sincerely, using plain English to explain context, intention and learning. This should support the visual work, not repeat it.

Some institutions also invite or require video introductions, particularly for performing arts programmes. These may include recordings of performances, rehearsals or personal introductions. Advisers can help students ensure that these are:

- Technically clear (well-lit, audible, appropriately framed).
- Professionally presented (attire, tone and setting considered).
- Honest representations of the student's current level, rather than overly polished productions.

Finally, students should be reminded that a strong portfolio reflects not only ability but also potential. Admissions staff are often looking for students who are open to growth, experimentation and feedback – qualities that can be conveyed just as powerfully through sketchbook pages as through final pieces.

By helping students select and present their creative work with confidence and intentionality, advisers can demystify what is often a high-stakes part of the international application process – and ensure that creative applicants are evaluated on the full merit of their ideas and imagination.

Advising on the ethical use of AI tools

Artificial intelligence is increasingly woven into how students think, write and prepare for higher education. Tools like ChatGPT, Grammarly and AI-driven college essay generators are readily available – and for many applicants, tempting shortcuts in the face of high-stakes deadlines. While these platforms can offer helpful starting points, their use raises serious questions about authenticity, integrity and institutional trust. Advisers now face the challenge of helping students understand not only how AI works, but when and how its use is appropriate.

Admissions officers, particularly in the US and Canada, are alert to the rise of AI-generated content. Some universities have introduced policies or guidance on AI use; others are still developing their stance. What is clear, however, is that content which reads as generic, overly structured or lacking personal insight may raise red flags – whether or not it was produced by a tool.

However, recent research highlights the difficulty universities face in detecting AI-generated content, with tools only marginally more effective than guessing. This presents ethical challenges and reinforces the need for transparent adviser guidance on responsible use (CalMatters, 2023).

Advisers can play a vital role in shaping students' understanding of AI in the application process. This begins with open, non-judgemental conversations that acknowledge the appeal of AI while foregrounding the values of academic honesty and self-expression.

Helpful messages to reinforce:

- AI is not inherently dishonest – but using it to replace original thinking or pass off generated content as personal writing is problematic.
- Brainstorming is acceptable – students can use AI to explore ideas, generate possible themes or get unstuck at the planning stage.
- Writing must remain their own – the reflective, nuanced voice that admissions staff value is difficult to fake – and essential to retain.
- Editing tools should support clarity, not rewrite meaning – grammar checks are useful, but rewriting for tone or content risks losing authenticity.

Advisers may find it useful to introduce a scaffolded writing process that builds from brainstorming to outline to drafting. This gives students a clear sense of progression and ownership, reducing the likelihood of heavy reliance on AI tools.

Where students are tempted to use AI for speed or confidence, advisers can offer alternatives:

- Peer feedback or writing circles.
- Sample prompts and student models (with commentary) – similar to the case studies in this chapter.
- Focused one-to-one discussion around personal themes and values.

Finally, it is worth discussing the longer-term implications of over-reliance on AI. University study – especially in systems that emphasise independent research and critical thinking – demands genuine engagement with material. Students who outsource too much of their application writing may find themselves underprepared for the real intellectual challenges ahead.

By promoting transparency, guiding appropriate use and modelling ethical reflection, advisers can help students approach AI not as a crutch, but as a tool – one that supports, rather than substitutes, their own voice.

Final thoughts

In supporting students with international applications, advisers act not only as editors or facilitators, but as mentors – helping young people find clarity in their ambitions and confidence in their voice. While systems vary, the core of a standout application remains the same: authenticity, alignment and a thoughtful connection between past experiences and future aspirations.

This chapter has highlighted the diverse ways in which students are asked to present themselves beyond their grades – from reflective essays and letters of motivation to portfolios and independent learning. It has also explored the increasingly complex role of technology in shaping these narratives, and the responsibility advisers carry in modelling ethical and effective approaches.

4 Making your application stand out

Importantly, advisers don't need to have all the answers. What matters most is their ability to ask the right questions, to challenge superficial responses and to guide students in making informed, reflective choices that will resonate with international admissions teams.

As the next chapters will explore, creating a strong application is only one part of the journey. Understanding the differences between university systems worldwide – and how best to match students to the environments where they will thrive – is the next critical step in shaping successful global pathways.

Adviser checklist

Understanding international expectations
- [✓] Encourage students to reflect on what sets them apart beyond academic grades.
- [✓] Support development of a clear, authentic narrative in all application materials.

US college essays
- [✓] Help students choose specific, honest experiences rather than broad themes.
- [✓] Emphasise personal voice and reflection over polish.
- [✓] Guide students on supplementals by encouraging specific references to the institution.

Letters of motivation for Europe
- [✓] Ensure students research the course structure and entry expectations.
- [✓] Support a concise, well-structured letter that explains subject interest and future goals.
- [✓] Help students link past experiences to specific course content.

Extracurricular and super curricular activities
- [✓] Encourage students to identify meaningful activities and reflect on what they've learnt.
- [✓] Prioritise depth over breadth of involvement.
- [✓] Support integration of activities into applications in a relevant, concise way.

Academic enrichment
- [✓] Recommend courses or talks that align with students' subject interests.
- [✓] Emphasise reflection over certification.
- [✓] Encourage habits of independent learning that can be referenced in applications.

Creative applications and portfolios
- [✓] Clarify portfolio requirements early, including written components.
- [✓] Support students in showing development and originality through selected work.
- [✓] Guide appropriate presentation and structure for submissions.

Ethical use of AI
- [x] Discuss how AI can support planning or clarity without replacing original writing.
- [x] Reinforce the importance of authenticity and student ownership.
- [x] Suggest structured alternatives such as planning templates or peer feedback.

FURTHER INFORMATION

College Essay Guy – A free and paid resource offering essay guides, brainstorming tools and videos specifically for US college admissions. Particularly useful for narrative coaching.
www.collegeessayguy.com

FutureLearn – A UK-based MOOC platform featuring subject-specific short courses ideal for super curricular engagement.
www.futurelearn.com

Coursera and edX – Global platforms offering academic enrichment courses from top universities, including certificates that can support applications.
www.coursera.org
www.edx.org

The Common App Essay Prompts – Official writing prompts used in most US applications. Helpful for planning workshops or essay reviews.
www.commonapp.org/apply/essay-prompts

Gresham College Lectures – Free access to university-level lectures across a wide range of subjects; useful for inspiring academic curiosity.
www.gresham.ac.uk

5 Applications and standardised testing

This chapter will:

- Explain the purpose of standardised tests in international admissions and when they are required for UK students applying abroad.
- Provide a clear guide to the most commonly encountered exams, including SAT, ACT, IELTS, TOEFL, UCAT, LNAT, MAT, STEP and HPAT.
- Compare testing requirements across key destinations such as the US, Canada, Ireland, the Netherlands and Australia.
- Outline timelines, preparation strategies and how advisers can help students plan test registration, manage costs and access support.
- Explore test-optional routes and holistic admissions policies, helping advisers guide students in deciding whether to submit scores.

Introduction: Why tests matter (and when they don't)

Thinking about studying abroad can be exciting – a fresh start in a new country, a different academic culture and experiences that go far beyond the lecture theatre. But once the student starts looking into international universities, they might quickly realise that there's a bit more to the application process than writing a personal statement and picking your five choices on UCAS.

One of the first things many UK students encounter is the requirement to take a standardised test – a type of assessment used to measure academic readiness in a uniform way, regardless of where you went to school. These aren't part of the student's GCSEs or A levels. They're additional exams, usually set by international admissions bodies and they can vary depending on where you're applying and what you plan to study.

The good news? Not every student needs to take one. And for those who do, most of these tests are highly structured, well-supported and totally manageable with the right preparation and planning. Some universities (especially in the US) use them to compare applicants from different educational systems, while others (such as universities in Europe) may ask for them to prove their English-language skills (if English is not their first language) or assess readiness for specialist courses like Medicine, Law or Maths.

In this chapter, we'll guide you through the major standardised tests UK students may come across when applying abroad. We'll explain what each test is for, what it includes, how to register, what it costs – and how to approach it with confidence. Whether you're applying to a university in the US, Canada, Ireland, the Netherlands, Australia or beyond, this section is designed to help you feel informed, prepared and confident to advise the student.

Understanding global applications

When supporting a student who is considering studying abroad, one of the first shifts for teachers and advisers to navigate is how different the application process can be outside the UK. Unlike the structured, centralised approach of UCAS, most international systems are more decentralised, more varied – and often require earlier planning. What changes with an international application?

UCAS offers a relatively consistent process: one form, five choices, one personal statement. In contrast, overseas systems often differ by country – and even by institution. The level of variation can feel daunting to students, especially if they are the first in their school or family to explore this route.

The standardised test guide

Advisers can use this section as a quick-reference overview of the key international standardised tests UK students may need to sit when applying abroad. For each entry, you'll find the test's purpose, scoring structure, sections, where and how it's taken, approximate cost and guidance on resources and preparation.

Where do standardised tests fit in?

Standardised tests are often used to ensure comparability across international education systems. As a UK adviser, you might be asked about a range of unfamiliar assessments – from the SAT to the TOEFL. These tests can be:

- Mandatory (e.g. SAT for some US universities).
- Optional but recommended (particularly at test-optional institutions in the US).
- Course-specific (e.g. UCAT for Medicine, LNAT for Law).

Some universities also require proof of English proficiency – even for native English speakers – especially if A levels alone are not considered sufficient evidence.

Adviser insight: What to emphasise
- Start early: Year 11 or Lower Sixth is the best time to begin serious research. Application deadlines abroad can fall months before UCAS.
- Build timelines: Students will need to juggle personal statements, essays, test prep and school commitments – helping them create a realistic plan is crucial.
- Understand the landscape: Not all students will need tests, but knowing which systems ask for what (and when) will allow you to guide them more confidently.

Advisers can use the next section to better understand the most widely used standardised tests that UK students may be required to take when applying abroad. The most important tests fall into three broad categories: general academic aptitude, English-language proficiency and subject-specific entrance tests. Below is a more detailed explanation of a few of the most commonly encountered assessments.

SAT (Scholastic Assessment Test) is a standardised test commonly required by US universities (but sometimes by others, such as those in Asia, who 'piggyback' on the system to assess international students). It measures evidence-based reading and writing, alongside mathematics. Scored out of 1600, the SAT is used to benchmark academic readiness. A score of 1300+ is typically competitive for selective universities. The test can be taken at authorised international centres, and is offered multiple times a year. Preparation is best done using official materials provided by the College Board or through free platforms like Khan Academy. It is important that students sit the SAT in Year 12 to allow time for a retake if needed.

ACT (American College Testing). An alternative to the SAT, the ACT includes sections on English, Maths, Reading and Science, with an optional writing component. The ACT is scored out of 36 and is accepted by all US universities. Some students prefer it for its straightforward structure and inclusion of scientific reasoning. Like the SAT, it can be taken at international centres and is offered several times annually.

IELTS (International English Language Testing System). The IELTS is the most widely used English-language proficiency test for UK students applying to international universities. It assesses listening, reading, writing and speaking, with each section scored from 0 to 9. Most institutions require a minimum score of 6.5 or 7.0. The speaking component is conducted face-to-face (or occasionally via web-based conferencing system) with an examiner. The test is offered frequently at centres across the UK and abroad.

TOEFL (Test of English as a Foreign Language). The TOEFL is another English proficiency exam, often preferred by institutions in the US and Canada. It follows a similar format to IELTS but is internet-based. The total score is out of 120. TOEFL is ideal for students comfortable with digital exams, and preparation materials are available online.

UCAT (University Clinical Aptitude Test). The UCAT is used by UK and some international universities for Medicine and Dentistry applications. In recent years, it has also been adopted by a growing number of institutions outside the UK – including medical schools in Australia, New Zealand and even Thailand – who recognise its potential as a standardised assessment for clinical reasoning and decision-making. It has been the preferred replacement for the BMAT (Biomedical Admissions Test), which was recently discontinued. It assesses a range of cognitive abilities and professional behaviours. The test includes sections such as Verbal Reasoning, Quantitative Reasoning and Situational Judgement, with scores ranging from 300–900 per section. It must be taken in the summer before Year 13. Preparation through timed practice is essential.

LNAT (Law National Aptitude Test). Required by some Law faculties in the UK and abroad, the LNAT evaluates a student's critical reading and argumentative writing. It consists of a multiple-choice comprehension section and an essay. While the multiple-choice is scored out of 42, the essay is reviewed qualitatively by admissions tutors. It's recommended students begin preparing during Year 12 through reading and discussion of current affairs and legal issues.

MAT (Mathematics Admissions Test). The MAT is used by universities such as Oxford and Imperial College London for courses involving mathematics and computer science. It consists of long-form problem-solving questions designed to assess mathematical thinking, not just memorised procedures. It is marked out of 100, with a score of 60+ considered strong. The test is sat in schools under exam conditions, typically in November. Preparation involves working through past papers available on university websites.

STEP (Sixth Term Examination Paper). STEP is an advanced maths exam required by a small number of universities, including Cambridge and Warwick. It is designed to test mathematical insight, rigour and creativity through complex extended questions. Students take one or more papers depending on their course requirements. Graded S, 1, 2, 3 or U, it is usually taken in June after A levels. Preparation is demanding and best undertaken with structured practice and support from maths teachers.

TMUA (Test of Mathematics for University Admission). The TMUA is used by several UK universities to assess mathematical thinking and logic. It has two multiple-choice papers: mathematical reasoning and mathematical thinking. Scored out of 9.0, a competitive applicant typically achieves 6.0 or above. While this test and the STEP are not known to be required by universities outside of the UK, a strong performance in the assessments is likely to strengthen an international application.

HPAT (Health Professions Admission Test – Ireland). The HPAT is required for students applying to undergraduate Medicine in the Republic of Ireland. It evaluates problem-solving, interpersonal understanding and abstract reasoning. The test is multiple-choice and scored on a scaled system. Preparation courses are available, though careful practice using sample questions can also be effective. The test is typically taken in February.

GED (General Educational Development). The GED is a UK-based high school equivalency exam, rarely used by UK students, but sometimes relevant for mature applicants. It covers language arts, maths, science and social studies. Each subject is scored out of 200, with 145 required to pass. It is accepted by some US colleges and universities internationally – especially in Australia. It can be taken online or in test centres.

Gaokao, ENEM and other national exams. These are country-specific university entrance exams, such as China's Gaokao or Brazil's ENEM. While not sat by UK students, some international universities – including a few in the UK – accept results from these tests for direct entry, particularly when a student has been educated abroad. UK advisers should be aware of these qualifications, as they may encounter a student who transfers to their school for the sixth form.

[NB: The STEP, MAT and TMUA are specialist maths tests mainly used by UK universities such as Cambridge, Oxford, Imperial and Warwick. Outside the UK, some institutions may consider them as part of an application which is why they have been included here. The National University of Singapore and Nanyang Technological University, for example, are known to accept strong STEP scores, while universities like TU Delft and the University of Amsterdam may also take them into account for maths-intensive degrees. Recognition is limited, and these tests are not formal entry requirements internationally, but they can still support an application where maths ability is key. Always check individual university guidance before including them.]

Standardised tests: At a glance

Further details on each test, including costs and test centres, can be found in Table 5.1 (overleaf).

Planning and preparation

Advisers play a key role in helping students build realistic, well-paced plans for testing. Standardised tests often take place outside regular school schedules, and with different deadlines for each country or institution, careful coordination is essential – particularly if students are preparing for more than one test or application route.

Ideally, conversations about testing should begin in Year 11 or early in Year 12. This gives students time to explore their options, choose the most suitable tests for their goals, and begin preparing with confidence. Starting early also leaves room for retakes if needed, and allows students to collect other key documents like teacher references, predicted grades and school transcripts well in advance.

Many students underestimate how far in advance test registration needs to happen. Booking is usually done through official websites, with students creating their own accounts, uploading ID, selecting a test centre and paying a fee – or applying for a waiver, where available. While some tests like the MAT or TMUA may be sat in school, most international tests such as the SAT or IELTS require attendance at approved centres, often on weekends or holidays.

Balancing test preparation with A level or IB study is another common concern. Encourage students to integrate preparation into their existing revision habits, rather than relying solely on last-minute cramming or expensive tutoring. Using official past papers, free online resources or low-cost prep materials is often enough – especially if students practise under timed conditions.

When it comes to retakes, timing and strategy matter. A single retake can be worthwhile if the student is motivated and can make meaningful improvements, but there is little benefit in repeating a test several times with no plan to change their approach. Some universities, particularly in the US, use a 'superscore' policy – considering the best section scores from multiple test sittings – which can work to a student's advantage.

Throughout the process, the most valuable role an adviser can play is to provide steady, structured support. Helping students build a timeline, avoid unnecessary pressure and understand how test results fit into the broader application can make all the difference to their confidence and clarity.

Costs, access and support

Standardised testing often comes with a financial cost, and for some students, this may be a source of anxiety or even a barrier to applying abroad. While many UK students are unfamiliar with the idea of paying to take an admissions test, this is a routine part of international university applications. Most tests charge a fee for

TABLE 5.1 Standardised tests

Test	Purpose	Scoring	Sections	Where it's sat	Typical cost	Commonly required by
SAT	General undergraduate admissions (esp. US)	400–1,600 (800 maths, 800 Reading/writing)	Reading, writing, maths	International test centres	£90–£120	US, Canada, some Europe/Asia
ACT	Alternative to SAT	1–36 (average of 4 sections)	English, maths, reading, science (+ Essay)	International test centres	£90–£130	US, some Canada/Asia
IELTS	English proficiency	0–9 per section (6.5–7.5 often required)	Listening, reading, writing, speaking	UK/global test centres	£200–£220	Most global universities
TOEFL	English proficiency (esp. North America)	Out of 120 (90+ typical)	Reading, listening, speaking, writing	Online or test centres	~£200	US, Canada, some Europe
Duolingo English Test	Online alternative to IELTS/TOEFL	Out of 160 (110–130 accepted)	Adaptive questions + video interview	Online only	~£50	Some US/EU universities
UCAT	Medicine/Dentistry aptitude test	300–900 per section (2,600+ competitive) + SJT band 1–4	Verbal reasoning, decision-making, quant, abstract, situational judgement	Pearson VUE centres	£70 UK/£115 int.	UK, Australia, NZ (Medicine/Dentistry)
LNAT	Law aptitude test	MCQ out of 42 + essay (unscored)	Reading comprehension, essay	Pearson VUE centres	£75 UK/£120 int.	Some UK and international Law schools
MAT	Mathematics admissions	Out of 100 (60+ strong)	Maths problems (no calculator)	Authorised school/test centre	~£50–£75	Oxford, Imperial, others
STEP	Advanced maths	Grades S, 1, 2, 3, U	Extended maths problems	School or centre	~£75	Cambridge, Warwick, others
TMUA	Maths admissions test	Out of 9.0 (6.0+ strong)	Maths and logic	School/test centre	~£50	Durham, others
HPAT (Ireland)	Medicine in Ireland	Varies; scaled score	Verbal, logic, interpersonal	Ireland/test centres	~€150	Irish universities (Medicine)
GED	High school equivalency (rarely used by UK students)	100–200 per subject (145 pass)	RLA, maths, science, social studies	Online or US/international centres	£100+	US unis (esp. for mature/non-traditional applicants)
Gaokao, ENEM, others	National exams (China, Brazil, etc.)	Country-specific	Country-specific	Country-specific	Varies	Used for direct entry to some UK/international universities

registration, and some also apply additional charges for late booking, rescheduling or sending results to multiple institutions.

The costs vary. English-language tests such as IELTS or TOEFL are among the more expensive, typically priced between £200 and £220. The SAT and ACT are slightly less, usually around £90 to £130, while subject-specific tests like the MAT, STEP or TMUA tend to cost around £50 to £75. Payment is usually made online at the time of registration, and students may need access to a debit or credit card.

While these fees are standard in international admissions, they can still pose a barrier for students from low-income households. According to data from the College Board (2023), disparities in test participation and performance are closely linked to socioeconomic background, with students from under-resourced schools often underperforming compared to their peers. Typically, parents of students from the independent sector of schools would employ a tutor to assist in preparation. This highlights the importance of proactive support around both preparation and access for students from lower-income families. Many testing organisations offer fee waivers or reduced-cost schemes, and advisers play a critical role in flagging these opportunities early. Checking the relevant test website and ensuring documentation is submitted on time can make a significant difference in improving access.

Support can also come in the form of preparation materials. While commercial courses are widely available, they are not a requirement for success. Most official websites offer free or low-cost preparation materials, including full-length practice papers, test-taking tips and answer explanations. For many students, this is sufficient – particularly if they are motivated and have a quiet space in which to work.

Some schools also offer internal mentoring or peer study groups, which can make preparation more accessible. Encouraging a culture of open discussion about testing – including where students can find help – can demystify the process and reduce unnecessary pressure.

For advisers, the key message to communicate is that cost should not be a blocker. With planning, signposting and encouragement, students from all backgrounds can successfully prepare for and complete the tests they need, particularly when their determination is high.

Putting scores in context

For many students and their families, standardised test scores can seem like the definitive measure of whether a university application will succeed. In reality, scores are just one part of a broader picture – and increasingly, they are being interpreted with greater flexibility by admissions teams around the world.

Advisers can help demystify this by explaining how scores are used alongside academic grades, personal essays, teacher recommendations, extracurricular records and interviews. In many international systems – particularly in the US – applications are reviewed holistically. A strong test score can support a candidate, but it rarely guarantees admission on its own. Equally, a slightly weaker score can often be balanced out by compelling evidence of academic potential or personal character elsewhere in the application.

Research by Hiss and Franks (2014), in the NACAC report *Defining Promise*, found that students admitted to test-optional institutions performed just as well – and sometimes better — than those who submitted scores. The findings reinforce the value of a broader, more inclusive approach to university admissions.

This is especially important in test-optional or test-flexible environments, where students can choose whether to submit scores at all. Advisers should encourage students to consider submitting results if their scores are a clear strength relative to institutional averages, but also reassure them that choosing not to submit — when appropriate — will not automatically disadvantage their application.

In addition, advisers can guide students in understanding that a 'good' score is relative: what counts as competitive varies by country, course and university. For example, a score of 1300 on the SAT may be very strong for one institution and merely average for another. Helping students research target score ranges and interpret their results in context will build their confidence and support informed decisions.

Advisers should remind students that test scores are not personal judgements. They reflect a performance on a specific day, under timed conditions — not a measure of worth or potential. Encouraging a balanced view of scores, as one part of a larger academic journey, can ease pressure and promote a healthier, more sustainable approach to the entire application process.

Case study: Grace — choosing a test-optional route to study International Relations in the US

Grace, a Year 13 student at a London sixth-form college, had long been drawn to international affairs. With her strong academic record in politics, history and English literature, she set her sights on studying International Relations in the US — a field where the interdisciplinary and globally focused curriculum offered exactly what she was looking for.

But with A level exams looming, Grace felt stretched. Between coursework, predicted grades and preparing her application essays, the thought of adding SAT or ACT preparation — let alone test dates and logistics — felt overwhelming.

After researching her options and speaking with a school adviser, Grace decided to focus exclusively on applying to test-optional universities in the US. She prioritised institutions known for strong Political Science or International Studies programmes that did not require standardised testing, particularly for international applicants.

Her final list included:

- George Washington University, located in Washington, DC, offers deep links to policy institutions and has a long-standing test-optional policy.
- American University, also based in DC, is known for its School of International Service and its commitment to holistic admissions.
- Clark University in Massachusetts, a liberal arts college that values global citizenship and does not require SAT/ACT scores.
- Smith College, a women's college with a rigorous global studies programme and a test-optional approach since 2009.

> Instead of devoting time to test prep, Grace concentrated on her A levels and crafted tailored application essays. She highlighted her Model UN involvement, summer work at a local NGO, and her strong written communication skills – all highly relevant to international relations.
>
> By choosing the test-optional route, Grace reduced her workload and stress at a crucial time, while still targeting institutions that aligned with her academic goals. She received offers from three of her four choices, and ultimately accepted a place at American University, where she now majors in International Studies and interns part-time at a policy think tank in Washington.

Conclusion

For students planning to study abroad, standardised testing can seem like an unfamiliar and occasionally intimidating hurdle. Yet with the right guidance, these assessments become manageable steps in a broader application journey.

As an adviser, your role is pivotal. By helping students understand which tests are required, when to take them and how to prepare effectively, you empower them to navigate this process with clarity and confidence. Your support turns what may feel like a barrier into a bridge – opening access to opportunities that extend well beyond the classroom.

With early planning, realistic timelines and a balanced view of what these tests represent, standardised assessments become just one part of a much larger and more exciting journey into international education.

Adviser checklist

Start early: Ideally from Year 11

- [x] Encourage students to explore whether tests will be required for their preferred destinations or courses and, if yes, build a timeline that incorporates school deadlines, test registration and preparation.

Know which tests apply

- [x] General academic aptitude: SAT, ACT.
- [x] English-language proficiency: IELTS, TOEFL, Duolingo English Test.
- [x] Subject-specific entrance tests: UCAT, LNAT, MAT, STEP, TMUA, HPAT.
- [x] Clarify which tests are mandatory, optional or course-specific for each country.

Guide test selection
- [x] Support students in choosing between SAT and ACT based on content and testing style.
- [x] Explain when subject tests like UCAT or LNAT are needed for Medicine or Law.
- [x] Highlight alternatives for students applying to test-optional universities.

Support preparation
- [x] Recommend free or low-cost prep materials (e.g. Khan Academy, official test sites).
- [x] Help students incorporate practice into existing study routines.
- [x] Encourage timed practice under exam conditions, especially for maths-based tests.

Manage logistics
- [x] Remind students to register on time, especially for international test centres.
- [x] Explain how to access fee waivers or support schemes for eligible students.
- [x] Clarify documentation needs, such as photo ID or school transcripts.

Put scores in context
- [x] Reinforce that test results are one part of a holistic application.
- [x] Discuss score ranges for target universities to set realistic expectations.
- [x] Advise students on whether to submit scores at test-optional institutions.

Advise on retakes
- [x] Plan retake dates if needed, but only with a clear strategy for improvement.
- [x] Explain how superscoring works and when it may be advantageous.

Reduce pressure
- [x] Normalise the experience of feeling challenged by tests.
- [x] Share success stories from students who chose test-optional routes.
- [x] Encourage focus on the full application – essays, recommendations and school performance matter too.

Stay informed
- [x] Monitor updates to test formats or university policies (e.g. SAT digital transition, BMAT retirement).
- [x] Use university websites or platforms like BridgeU and Unifrog to track evolving requirements.

FURTHER INFORMATION

College Board – SAT and AP Registration: https://satsuite.collegeboard.org/sat

ACT – Test Information and Dates: https://www.act.org

IELTS – Test Details and Booking: https://www.ielts.org

TOEFL – Registration and Prep Resources: https://www.ets.org/toefl

Duolingo English Test – Practice and Scores: https://englishtest.duolingo.com

UCAT – UK Clinical Aptitude Test: https://www.ucat.ac.uk

LNAT – Law National Aptitude Test: https://lnat.ac.uk

TMUA – University Admissions Tests UK: https://esat-tmua.ac.uk/about-the-tests/tmua-test/

6 The European perspective

This chapter will:

- Explore the main opportunities and challenges for UK students considering study in Europe.
- Highlight key destinations, including typical costs, admission systems and language requirements.
- Cover practical issues such as visas, accommodation and part-time work regulations.
- Provide adviser-focused guidance for supporting students through the European application process.
- Point to reliable resources and official agencies for current information and further advice.

Introduction

Europe continues to offer a wealth of opportunities for UK students seeking to study overseas. From world-renowned universities such as the University of Amsterdam and Heidelberg University, to diverse course options and lower tuition fees, studying in Europe remains an appealing pathway. Despite changes to fee structures and visa arrangements, many European countries have adapted their systems to remain accessible and welcoming to international students.

Advisers have a crucial role to play in supporting students who are considering Europe as a study destination. It is essential to understand the specific systems, deadlines, language requirements and costs associated with different countries. Being aware of the practical challenges students may face, such as securing accommodation or navigating local application portals, is also important.

This chapter provides a country-by-country overview of key European destinations, highlighting the opportunities available and the points advisers need to consider when guiding students. Whether learners are drawn by English-taught courses, affordable living costs or specialist programmes, understanding the European higher education landscape will enable advisers to offer timely, informed and practical advice.

Practical tips for advisers

Supporting students who are considering studying in Europe requires a proactive, informed approach. Advisers can play a crucial role in helping students navigate the differences between education systems, entry requirements and living arrangements across a range of European countries.

Early planning is essential

Application deadlines for European universities can be significantly earlier than for UCAS applications, particularly for selective courses or programmes with limited places. Advisers should encourage students to begin researching their options at least a year in advance using platforms like Unifrog or BridgeU – where students using their search tools can enter their likely qualifications (such as A levels, BTECs or IB scores), and then match these to course entry requirements. Students can then categorise potential university options into three columns:

- Aspirational – where the entry requirements slightly exceed the student's predictions.
- Secure – where the student's predicted grades meet typical requirements.
- Safe – where the student is likely to exceed the entry requirements.

This system helps students to build a realistic and well-balanced short list of courses. It also enables advisers to review choices in a structured way and support students in making competitive applications which should include a clear 'backup' or insurance choice should their final examinations not go as well as expected. It is always wise to consider some European-based international foundation programmes to this end. There are many which are taught in English. These provide a possible pathway for students if their A level grades fall below the requisite C grade required by many European institutions.

For schools without access to platforms such as Unifrog or BridgeU – which are subscription-based, AI research tools are becoming an increasingly useful alternative. Free accounts on platforms like ChatGPT or Perplexity can help students begin exploring courses and universities by asking focused questions about subjects, destinations and entry criteria. These tools can provide direct links to universities' websites, which students should use to verify the information and check key details such as deadlines, documentation and language requirements.

It's also important to pay close attention to the specific documentation required by each institution.

Think about language requirements and tuition fees

Language considerations must be addressed early. While English-taught programmes are increasingly available across Europe, particularly in countries such as the Netherlands, Germany and Poland, students should not assume that daily life will always be conducted in English. Advisers should encourage students to assess their language skills realistically and to consider enrolling in introductory language courses if needed, both to support their academic success and to aid social integration.

Financial planning is another critical area. Although tuition fees in Europe are often lower than in the UK, the availability of financial support varies widely. See Chapter 10 for advice in this realm.

Research visa and work permit issues

International students are permitted to work part-time in most European countries, although conditions vary. In the Netherlands, students can work up to 16 hours per week during term time or full-time in the summer, but must obtain a work permit through their employer. In Germany, students may work 120 full days or 240 half-days per year without needing a special permit. France allows students to work up to 964 hours per year (approximately 20 hours per week), with the right to work automatically included with a student visa. In Spain, students can work 20 hours per week but must obtain separate authorisation linked to their studies.

In the Czech Republic, international students enrolled in accredited programmes may work up to 20 hours per week without a work permit, although Czech language skills are often needed for employment outside international companies. In Poland, students can work 20 hours per week during the academic year and full-time during holidays without needing a separate work permit, provided they hold a valid student residence permit.

Advisers should remind students that work opportunities may be limited by language barriers, permit processing times or specific local requirements, and that academic commitments should remain the priority. But the ability to work part-time while studying does provide a good supplement to living expenses. A more detailed summary of the rules for part-time work can also be found in Chapter 10.

Be strategic

Finally, advisers should help students think strategically about how a European degree fits into their long-term career plans. This may involve discussing professional accreditation, recognition of qualifications in the UK or the potential for postgraduate study either abroad or at home. By encouraging students to ask the right questions early, advisers can empower them to make well-informed, confident choices about studying in Europe.

Case study: Vishal's journey to studying Songwriting in Germany

Vishal had always dreamed of pursuing a career in music. After completing his BTEC Level 3 Diploma in Music Performance at college in the UK, he began researching international options for higher education. His passion was primarily for drumming, although he had recently started writing his own material and was keen to develop his songwriting skills further.

Rather than follow the traditional UK university route, Vishal discovered BIMM Institute – a specialist modern music school with campuses across Europe, including Berlin, Germany. BIMM Berlin offered a BA (Hons) in Songwriting, taught entirely in English, and provided a creative, industry-focused learning environment that immediately appealed to him.

One of the key advantages for Vishal was BIMM's flexible entry requirements. Unlike many traditional conservatoires, BIMM places greater emphasis on musical potential, passion and industry experience rather than formal qualifications alone. BTEC qualifications were fully accepted for entry onto the BA Songwriting course, providing a more accessible route for students who had chosen vocational pathways. Although Vishal was a confident drummer, he could not sight-read music fluently, which might have been a barrier at a more traditional conservatoire. However, BIMM focused on his creative abilities and his portfolio of original work during the application process, rather than requiring advanced sight-reading.

Vishal submitted a portfolio including recordings of his drumming and early songwriting projects. He also attended an online interview where he was able to discuss his musical influences, aspirations and commitment to developing as a songwriter. Shortly afterwards, he received an offer for the course.

Moving to Berlin opened up new creative and cultural opportunities for Vishal. The cost of living was manageable compared to London, and the city's vibrant music scene provided an inspiring backdrop to his studies. Through BIMM's strong industry connections, he was able to network with other musicians, perform live and start building a professional portfolio.

Vishal's experience highlights the growing number of flexible, specialist options available to students who wish to study-abroad. For advisers, it underlines the importance of looking beyond traditional academic pathways and recognising institutions like BIMM that value creativity, individuality and vocational qualifications such as BTECs. BIMM also operates campuses in Brighton and other UK cities, alongside Berlin, Hamburg and Dublin, giving students flexibility in choosing where to study.

Decision point

Vishal chose BIMM Berlin for its creative focus, flexible entry requirements and lower living costs. The English-taught BA in Songwriting and emphasis on portfolio work suited his strengths and career goals.

Adviser insight

This case shows how vocational qualifications like BTECs can support progression to specialist institutions. Advisers should consider non-traditional options for creative students with strong practical skills and artistic ambition.

Supporting UK students considering Europe

Studying in Europe offers UK students a range of advantages, but it also presents specific challenges that advisers need to be prepared for. Understanding the structure of different education systems, the key application processes and the practical considerations involved will enable advisers to provide informed and realistic guidance. Insights from the British Council highlight that students increasingly prioritise clarity of process, cost predictability and post-study work options when considering European destinations (British Council, 2022). This makes the adviser's role in demystifying country-specific pathways more critical than ever.

Study Abroad Made Simple

Watch out for early deadlines

Early preparation is essential. Application deadlines in some European countries are significantly earlier than those for UK universities, and the application process itself may involve additional steps such as entrance examinations, portfolio submissions or interviews. Advisers should familiarise themselves with the key portals and processes, such as Studielink in the Netherlands and uni-assist in Germany, to provide accurate advice.

Finally, advisers have an important role in ensuring that students use official, reliable resources when researching their options. Signposting students towards organisations such as DAAD (German Academic Exchange Service) and Nuffic (the Dutch organisation for internationalisation in education) can provide them with up-to-date and trustworthy information, reducing the risk of confusion or misinformation.

Supporting students who are considering Europe requires both attention to detail and a proactive approach. With the right information and careful planning, students can access a rich array of opportunities across the continent.

The Netherlands: One of the most popular destinations for international students

The Netherlands offers a wide range of high-quality, English-taught degree programmes across a variety of disciplines. Its welcoming approach to international students, relatively affordable tuition fees and strong global reputation make it an attractive option for those seeking to study-abroad.

Dutch universities are highly regarded internationally. The University of Amsterdam is particularly well known for humanities, social sciences and business studies, while Delft University of Technology enjoys a strong global reputation in engineering and technology fields. Many institutions offer a wide range of English-taught bachelor's and master's degrees, providing UK students with academic choice without the need for fluency in Dutch at the point of entry.

Nuffic, the Dutch organisation for internationalisation in education, provides a wealth of information on studying in the Netherlands, including advice on applications, funding and living in Dutch cities. Advisers should encourage students to make full use of this resource when planning their move. It remains the main source of information about equivalent UK qualifications and their acceptability (e.g. BTECs).

For UK students considering studying in the Netherlands, it's important to understand the differences between research universities and universities of applied sciences. Research universities offer academically rigorous, theory-driven degrees designed for students with strong A levels – usually three in relevant subjects – comparable to the Dutch VWO qualification. These bachelor's programmes typically last three years and are ideal for those interested in academic study or pursuing a master's or PhD. Teaching is focused on lectures, seminars and independent research.

In contrast, universities of applied sciences provide more vocational, career-focused education and usually accept a broader range of UK qualifications, including two A levels, BTECs or a mix of Level 3 qualifications, aligned with Dutch HAVO or MBO-4 levels. Bachelor's degrees here usually take four years and include practical work placements, industry projects and hands-on learning. While applied science graduates can progress to the workforce directly, they may need a bridging course to access academic master's degrees. This distinction allows students to choose a path that best suits their academic strengths, career goals and preferred learning style.

Applying to Dutch universities

Applications to Dutch universities are made through a centralised system known as Studielink. Students are advised to apply early, as deadlines can be significantly earlier than those in other European countries, particularly for courses with a limited number of places (known as numerus fixus courses). In addition to the Studielink application, some institutions may require a separate application or additional documentation, so it is important that students check the requirements of each university carefully.

Studielink functions more as a registry, compared to the UK's UCAS portal, which has much greater adviser input and linkage. For example, the centre does not have an overview of the candidates' applications on Studielink, and advisers can only see the progress of the application if the student provides the information. Centres have to certify predicted grades, but often a reference is not a requirement. Each university will charge €50–€100 per course application. So a considered approach is useful.

Tuition and accommodation

Tuition fees for UK students in the Netherlands are typically around €2,530 per year at public universities, although fees for non-EU students will be higher in most cases. Living costs vary depending on location but are generally lower than those in major UK cities. Students should expect to pay between €400 and €800 per month for private accommodation, depending on the city. Additional costs for food, transport and study materials are typically estimated at €1,000–€1,200 per month in total. Cities such as Amsterdam and Utrecht tend to be more expensive, while smaller towns like Groningen or Maastricht offer lower living costs.

Accommodation can present a challenge for students. The Netherlands is experiencing a significant housing shortage, with demand for both private rentals and student accommodation far exceeding supply. New rent control measures, introduced through the Affordable Rent Act in 2024, have placed limits on mid-range private rental prices; however, this has also led some private landlords to leave the rental market, reducing availability further. Students should be advised to begin their housing search as early as possible and to consider a range of options, including university-managed accommodation, private rentals and shared housing.

As well as value on tuition fees, the Netherlands remains generous with offers also. Dutch universities often make conditional offers based on official teacher-predicted grades and will tend to accept three A levels, provided they are at grade C or above – so the pressure we witness to achieve top grades with some Russell Group universities in the UK does not exist to the same extent here.

Language and visa requirements

Language remains an important consideration. Although degree programmes may be delivered entirely in English, students will find that a basic understanding of Dutch is extremely helpful for day-to-day life. Some universities offer introductory language courses to support international students with integration into local communities (e.g. the University of Groningen).

UK students now require a visa and residence permit to study in the Netherlands. For courses longer than 90 days, universities typically apply for these documents on the student's behalf once an offer is accepted. Students should check specific timelines carefully and ensure that all supporting documents, such as proof of sufficient funds and health insurance, are prepared early.

Germany: A high-quality, affordable higher education system

Germany remains a consistently popular choice for UK students. With no tuition fees charged at most public universities and a growing number of English-taught courses, Germany provides a high-quality alternative to traditional study pathways within the UK. Its universities enjoy strong international reputations, particularly in fields such as engineering, natural sciences, social sciences and business. Given the low or non-existent tuition fees, German universities tend to be a little more selective on entry, compared to the UK or other European countries.

German universities are consistently ranked among the best in Europe. Heidelberg University, Germany's oldest university, has an outstanding global reputation for medicine, life sciences and humanities, while the Technical University of Munich is particularly well regarded for engineering, technology and natural sciences. Both institutions, alongside many others across Germany, offer a wide range of research opportunities and maintain strong industry links, enhancing students' employability prospects after graduation.

How to apply

Applications to German universities can vary depending on the institution and the student's chosen programme. Many universities require students to apply directly, although some use a centralised service called uni-assist to process applications. Advisers should remind students to check whether their intended course demands additional entrance qualifications, such as subject-specific A levels or proof of a university entrance qualification (Abitur equivalence).

Language requirements

Students may also need to demonstrate language proficiency, either in English or German, depending on the course requirements. German public universities often make offers to candidates with a C grade or above at A level. Acceptability of BTEC needs to be checked separately, but it is not as well regarded overall.

While English-taught programmes are increasingly common, especially at master's level, students applying for undergraduate courses may find that knowledge of German is essential. Some universities offer foundation programmes or preparatory courses (e.g. Freiburg) to help international students strengthen their language and academic skills before beginning full degree studies.

Living costs and visa issues

Living costs in Germany are relatively low compared to the UK, although students should factor in expenses such as health insurance, which is mandatory for all students. Many international students also benefit from reduced public transport fares and discounted access to cultural events through their student status.

Students should be encouraged to make use of DAAD, the German Academic Exchange Service, which offers comprehensive guidance on courses, scholarships and practical matters such as accommodation and visas. Early planning is essential, as application deadlines can vary and some programmes may have limited places for non-EU students.

UK students must now apply for a student visa and residence permit to study in Germany. The application process usually requires proof of admission to a recognised institution, financial means and evidence of health insurance coverage. Students should be encouraged to begin the visa application process well in advance, as processing times can vary.

France: A tradition of academic excellence

France remains a leading destination for UK students seeking a high-quality, internationally recognised education. With a strong tradition in academic excellence, a growing number of English-taught programmes and comparatively low tuition fees at public institutions, France offers a rich and varied higher education landscape.

France is home to some of Europe's most prestigious universities. Sorbonne University in Paris is renowned for arts, humanities and sciences, while Sciences Po is highly respected for its programmes in Political Science, International Relations and Law. Both institutions, along with a wide range of others across the country, provide opportunities for academic excellence and career development in an international environment.

How to apply

UK students remain eligible to apply for French universities following the UK's departure from the EU, although they are now classed as international students for fee and visa purposes. Applications to French universities can vary depending on the type of institution and the course chosen. For undergraduate courses at public universities, students typically apply directly or through the centralised Parcoursup system.

Students considering France should begin their planning early, as administrative procedures such as visa applications, proof of language proficiency and registration with local authorities can take time to complete. Advisers can direct students to Campus France, the national agency promoting French higher education abroad, which provides detailed information on courses, admissions and student life.

Selective institutions such as the Grandes Écoles, which specialise in areas such as engineering, business and political science, often have separate admissions processes that may include competitive entrance examinations. Advisers should guide students to check individual entry requirements carefully, as the admissions timeline and procedures can differ significantly from UK systems.

UK students are required to apply for a student visa to study in France. Applications are typically made through the Etudes en France platform, and students must show proof of admission, sufficient financial resources and health insurance. Advisers should remind students that visa processing can take several weeks, particularly during peak periods.

Tuition fees and language requirements

Tuition fees at French public universities are relatively modest by international standards. For non-EU students (including UK students), undergraduate courses typically cost around €2,770 per year, plus some additional administrative fees. EU students pay lower statutory fees of around €170 per year. Some institutions choose to waive the higher rate for certain students. Private institutions and Grandes Écoles generally charge significantly higher fees, although scholarships and financial aid schemes are often available to international students. Living costs vary by city, with Paris being considerably more expensive than regional towns and cities. For more detailed information on fees and scholarships, see Chapter 10.

An increasing number of courses in France are offered entirely or partly in English, particularly at master's level. However, at the undergraduate level, English-taught options are less widespread, and students may need to demonstrate French language proficiency for many courses. Even where programmes are taught in English, a good working knowledge of French is highly beneficial for daily life, part-time work and integration into the local community. Many universities offer language support services to help international students improve their French skills alongside their studies.

Spain: An increasingly attractive option

Spain is becoming popular for UK students seeking an affordable, high-quality university education combined with a vibrant cultural experience. With a wide range of public and private institutions, comparatively low living costs and a growing number of English-taught courses, Spain offers a compelling alternative to study within the UK.

Spain is home to several highly regarded universities. The University of Barcelona is consistently ranked among the top institutions in Europe for arts, humanities and science subjects, while IE University, with campuses in Madrid and Segovia, offers a strong portfolio of Business, Law and International Relations programmes taught in English.

How to apply

UK students remain eligible to apply to Spanish universities, although they are now classed as international applicants. In most cases, students will need to have their UK qualifications officially recognised through a process known as homologación, which confirms that their school-leaving qualifications are equivalent to the Spanish bachillerato. The homologación process can take several months, so early preparation is essential. Applications are usually made directly to individual universities, although some regions also operate centralised admission platforms (e.g. UNEDasiss).

Advisers can guide students towards official resources such as the Spanish Ministry of Education and individual university admissions offices for the most up-to-date information on entry requirements, visa procedures and available programmes.

Tuition fees

Tuition fees in Spain are relatively modest, particularly at public universities, where undergraduate fees typically range from €750 to €2,500 per year, depending on the region and course. Private universities tend to charge higher fees. Living costs are generally lower than in the UK, although cities such as Madrid and Barcelona are more expensive than smaller regional centres.

Language and visa requirements

While the majority of undergraduate courses in Spain are taught in Spanish, there is a growing number of English-taught programmes, particularly in fields such as business, engineering and international relations. Students interested in English-taught courses should research options carefully, as availability can vary widely between institutions. Even where courses are delivered in English, knowledge of Spanish is highly recommended to support daily life, part-time employment and integration into the community. Many universities offer Spanish language courses to help international students build their language skills.

UK students must obtain a student visa to study in Spain for courses lasting longer than 90 days. Visa applications should be submitted through the Spanish consulate, and students must provide proof of enrolment, financial means, health insurance and, in some cases, a criminal record check. Early preparation is recommended to avoid delays.

Czech Republic: Prestige with more flexible options

The Czech Republic is emerging as a popular destination for UK students, particularly those interested in studying medicine, dentistry and veterinary science at more affordable rates than in the UK. With a long academic tradition, a growing number of English-taught programmes and a relatively low cost of living, the country offers an appealing study option within Europe.

Charles University in Prague, founded in 1348, is one of the oldest and most prestigious universities in Central Europe. It offers a range of highly respected English-taught programmes, particularly in the fields of medicine and sciences. Several other universities across the country, including Masaryk University in Brno, also offer strong English-language degree options.

How to apply

UK students remain eligible to apply to Czech universities, although they are now considered non-EU applicants and may be subject to different fee structures and visa requirements. Applications are typically made directly to individual universities. For many competitive courses, particularly in medical fields, students must pass entrance examinations in subjects such as biology, chemistry and physics. Early preparation for these assessments is strongly advised.

Students interested in studying in the Czech Republic should plan early, particularly if they intend to apply for medicine-related courses where competition is fierce. Advisers should encourage students to seek information directly from university admissions offices and to check visa, insurance and entrance exam requirements well in advance of their intended start date.

Tuition fees and language issues

Public universities in the Czech Republic generally charge no tuition fees for courses taught in Czech. However, for programmes delivered in English, tuition fees apply. Fees for English-taught degrees are relatively affordable compared to UK standards, typically ranging from €4,650 to €13,950 per year, depending on the subject and institution. Living costs are also low, with accommodation, transport and daily expenses costing considerably less than in the UK.

English-taught programmes are widely available, particularly at master's level and in specialised fields such as medicine, engineering and business. At undergraduate level, options are more limited but steadily growing. While it is possible to study entirely in English, learning some basic Czech is strongly recommended to enhance everyday life, part-time work opportunities and integration into the local community.

Visa requirements

UK students require a long-term residence visa for study purposes in the Czech Republic. Applications should be made at a Czech embassy and typically involve proof of university acceptance, financial self-sufficiency, accommodation arrangements and health insurance. Processing times can be lengthy, so early submission is essential.

Poland: An affordable option

Poland is an increasingly popular destination for UK students seeking high-quality education at an affordable cost. With a strong academic tradition, a wide range of English-taught programmes and some of the lowest living expenses in Europe, Poland offers a compelling alternative for those considering studying abroad.

The University of Warsaw, Poland's largest university, is highly respected internationally, particularly for its programmes in humanities, social sciences and natural sciences. Other institutions such as Jagiellonian University in Kraków also offer a broad range of English-taught degrees and have strong international reputations.

How to apply

UK students are eligible to apply to Polish universities as international applicants and must now meet visa and residence permit requirements following Brexit. Most applications are made directly to individual universities, although some institutions participate in national-level platforms for specific courses. Entry requirements vary but often include school-leaving qualifications equivalent to A levels, and in some cases, entrance examinations for competitive subjects such as medicine.

Students considering study in Poland should be advised to research the recognition of degrees for future career plans, particularly if they intend to return to the UK to work in regulated professions such as medicine or law. Early planning around visas, insurance and accommodation is also important to ensure a smooth transition.

Tuition fees

Tuition fees for English-taught programmes in Poland are highly competitive, typically ranging from €2,000 to €6,000 per year, depending on the institution and subject. Public universities charge no tuition fees for courses taught in Polish, but fees apply for English-medium programmes. Living costs are low compared to the UK, with affordable accommodation, food and transport contributing to an overall lower financial burden for students.

Language and visa requirements

English-taught degrees are widely available across disciplines such as Medicine, Engineering, IT, Business and International Relations. Many universities have expanded their English-language offerings significantly over the past decade, making it possible for students to complete full undergraduate or postgraduate degrees without needing proficiency in Polish. Nevertheless, learning some basic Polish is strongly encouraged to assist with daily life and integration into the wider community.

UK students studying in Poland must apply for a national visa (D-type) for stays exceeding 90 days. Required documents usually include an offer of admission, proof of funds, health insurance and evidence of accommodation. Students should be advised to check embassy guidelines carefully and allow ample time for visa processing.

Case study: Niamh — following a flexible path into a hospitality degree in Spain

Background

Niamh left school at the end of Year 12 without completing any Level 3 qualifications. Though she had enjoyed parts of her studies, ongoing mental health challenges and a lack of interest in purely academic subjects prompted her to step away. Over the next year, she worked in a local café and later a boutique hotel, gaining first-hand experience of the hospitality industry. She thrived in fast-paced, customer-focused roles and soon became keen to turn that interest into a long-term career.

Decision point

Returning to full-time study in the UK didn't feel like the right fit. Instead, Niamh explored alternative routes to university. After researching online and speaking to her careers adviser, she discovered that the General Educational Development (GED) test – a US-based high school equivalency – was accepted by several international universities. She was particularly drawn to the Universidad Europea de Valencia, which offered a bachelor's in Tourism and Leisure Management taught entirely in English. The course combined practical modules in hospitality and event planning with internships in the tourism sector, making it a strong match for her ambitions.

'I wanted something hands-on that didn't feel like school again', Niamh says. 'The idea of studying somewhere new and getting real experience at the same time really appealed to me.'

Adviser insight

Universidad Europea has a flexible admissions policy and does consider applications from GED holders, especially for vocationally aligned, internationally focused courses. Applicants should be prepared to provide supporting materials such as a personal statement, academic transcripts, a CV and proof of English proficiency.

Fees for this programme were around €9,000 per year at the time Niamh applied, with options for instalment plans. While this is broadly in line with UK university tuition fees, the lower cost of living in Valencia and the course's strong emphasis on employability were key factors in Niamh's decision.

Comparison with UK-based options

In the UK, students interested in hospitality management without traditional Level 3 qualifications might consider Access to HE courses or vocational qualifications such as a BTEC. While these routes can lead to university, they typically require at least one additional year of study. For some students – particularly those who are motivated, independent and looking for a fresh start – international options like Niamh's can offer a faster, more tailored route into higher education.

Table 6.1 summarises the key points to consider when applying to European universities and outlines the advantages and disadvantages of each country's system.

Conclusion

Europe continues to offer a wealth of opportunities for UK students, with a diverse range of high-quality, affordable study options across many countries. Data from the UNESCO Institute for Statistics confirms that Europe remains one of the top destinations for internationally mobile students, particularly at undergraduate level (UNESCO, 2025). This reinforces the importance of strategic, well-informed advising for UK students exploring continental options.

Advisers can empower students to explore the full range of opportunities Europe offers by providing accurate information, encouraging early preparation and supporting realistic decision-making. With the right guidance, students can gain not only an excellent education but also valuable international experience that will serve them well in their future careers.

6 The European perspective

TABLE 6.1 An overview of European applications

Country	Tuition fees (approx.)	Language of instruction	Advantages	Disadvantages
Netherlands	€2,530/year (public)	English-taught widely.	High-quality degrees; strong international links; early career opportunities.	Housing shortage; earlier deadlines; moderate living costs.
Germany	Mostly free (public universities)	English options growing, German for many undergraduates.	No tuition fees; excellent reputation in sciences and engineering.	German language often required; visa needed.
France	€2,770/year (public)	Mainly French, growing English-taught options.	Affordable public tuition; prestigious institutions.	French needed for daily life; complex application processes.
Spain	€750–€2,500/year (public)	Mainly Spanish, some English-taught degrees.	Lower tuition and living costs; growing English programmes.	Homologación process; fewer English-taught undergraduates.
Czech Republic	£4,000–£12,000/year (English-taught courses)	English widely available for medical and technical fields.	Affordable education; good reputation in medicine.	Entrance exams common; visa processing times.
Poland	€2,000–€6,000/year (English-taught courses)	English widely available.	Very low living costs; wide range of English degrees.	Language barrier outside university; check degree recognition.

75

Adviser checklist

Start planning early
- [x] Encourage research at least 12 months ahead of application deadlines.
- [x] Use tools like Unifrog, BridgeU or AI platforms (e.g. ChatGPT, Perplexity) to explore options.
- [x] Help students categorise choices as Aspirational, Secure or Safe.

Understand national differences
- [x] Familiarise yourself with key systems like Studielink (Netherlands), uni-assist (Germany), Parcoursup (France) and UNEDasiss (Spain).
- [x] Check whether additional steps such as entrance exams, portfolio submissions or interviews are required.
- [x] Review documentation needs (e.g. certified transcripts, English-language tests, proof of funds).

Clarify tuition and living costs
- [x] Compare tuition fees across countries – many offer lower or no fees at public universities.
- [x] Highlight differences between EU and non-EU fees post-Brexit.
- [x] Help students build a full budget: tuition, accommodation, insurance, travel and visa costs.

Address language requirements
- [x] Discuss whether the course is fully English-taught and what level of local language will be needed for everyday life.
- [x] Encourage students to take beginner courses in the destination language if relevant.
- [x] Check whether universities offer language support.

Explain visa processes
- [x] Guide students through visa timelines, health insurance and financial documentation.
- [x] Reinforce that visa processing can be slow – start early and stay organised.
- [x] Highlight key visa platforms (e.g. Etudes en France, Czech consulates, Polish D-visas).

Explore part-time work rules
- [x] Clarify student work entitlements (hours per week, type of permit needed).
- [x] Check how language skills may impact job opportunities.
- [x] Emphasise that academic success must remain the priority.

Highlight flexible entry pathways
- [x] Support applications to international foundation years or applied science routes where A levels are lower or BTECs are the main qualification.
- [x] Consider universities and institutions with vocational or portfolio-based entry, such as BIMM or Universidad Europea.

6 The European perspective

Link study to career progression
- ☑ Discuss professional recognition of European degrees in the UK and beyond.
- ☑ Explore postgraduate study options and long-term career impact.
- ☑ Encourage students to evaluate employability outcomes and industry connections.

Use official resources
- ☑ Signpost students to reliable sources (e.g. DAAD, Nuffic, Campus France, Study in Spain, Go Poland).
- ☑ Avoid reliance on unofficial rankings or second-hand advice.
- ☑ Verify details such as course duration, fees, language and application process via university websites.

FURTHER INFORMATION

For students considering studying in Europe, and for advisers supporting them, the following organisations and official resources provide up-to-date information on courses, applications, funding and student life:

Nuffic (Netherlands) – Comprehensive information on studying in the Netherlands, including Studielink guidance, funding and accommodation advice.
www.nuffic.nl/en

DAAD – German Academic Exchange Service (Germany) – Course database, scholarship information and practical advice for international students.
www.daad.de/en

Campus France (France) – Official resource for studying in France, including application procedures, visa guidance and scholarships.
www.campusfrance.org/en

Study in Spain – Government-supported portal offering advice on Spanish universities, degree recognition (homologación) and living in Spain.
www.studyinspain.info

Study in the Czech Republic – Information on English-taught programmes, entrance requirements and living costs.
www.studyin.cz

Go Poland – National Agency for Academic Exchange (Poland) – Official guidance on studying in Poland, scholarships and student visas.
www.go-poland.pl

UK Government – Studying Abroad – Guidance for UK nationals studying in the EU, including visa requirements and healthcare advice.
www.gov.uk/guidance/study-in-the-european-union

7 Exploring the East: Applying to Asia, New Zealand and Australia

This chapter will:

- Explore international university options in Australia, New Zealand and Asia, including how systems differ from UCAS.
- Explain key academic requirements, including the use of actual grades, ATAR conversion in Australia and the role of English-language tests.
- Introduce TAFE colleges as a vocational alternative for students, particularly those with BTEC qualifications.
- Compare application routes, timelines and recognition of UK qualifications across regions, with practical advice for planning.
- Highlight how advisers and parents can guide students through decisions, documentation and cultural readiness.

Why Asia and Australasia are worth considering

Asia and Australia offer exciting alternatives to studying in the UK or US.
If you're exploring your options for higher education, it's worth looking further afield. These regions are home to some of the world's most innovative and highly ranked universities. They also offer the chance to live and study in fast-changing global environments.

You don't need to speak another language to study in these regions.
Most courses in Australia are taught in English. In parts of Asia, including Hong Kong, Singapore and increasingly Japan, you'll find a growing number of degrees delivered entirely in English. You'll still need to meet academic entry requirements – and sometimes language ones too – but you don't always need to speak the local language fluently to get started.

Living costs and tuition fees can be lower than in the UK.
Studying abroad doesn't always mean paying more. In many Australian states, tuition fees for international students are competitive and scholarships are widely available. In Asia, some governments actively fund international students through grants or bursaries, especially in science and technology subjects. When comparing the full cost of study – tuition, housing, travel – it can often be less expensive than staying in the UK.

7 Exploring the East: Applying to Asia, New Zealand and Australia

Studying abroad can give you a serious career advantage.
Employers value graduates who are adaptable, culturally aware and internationally minded. If you're thinking about a global career, experience in Asia or Australia shows that you're willing to take on a challenge and step outside your comfort zone. International networks built at university can be career assets for years to come.

What advisers and teachers can do:
- Encourage early research into international study options.
- Compare fees, course content and post-study work opportunities.
- Discuss whether the student is open to living far from home for an extended time.
- Help balance practical questions (e.g. visas, insurance, accommodation) with academic fit.

Australia's application system: Structured, but grade-focused

Applying to university in Australia is different from using UCAS – and it's all about your final results.
Australian universities don't usually make offers based on predicted grades. Instead, they wait for your actual results before making a decision. This means most UK-based applicants apply after receiving their A level or BTEC results.

There's no single national application system.
In Australia, each state or territory manages its own university admissions through a central portal. For example:

- UAC (Universities Admissions Centre) – New South Wales and ACT;
- VTAC (Victorian Tertiary Admissions Centre) – Victoria;
- QTAC, SATAC, TISC – for Queensland, South Australia and Western Australia, respectively.

Some universities also accept direct applications from international students. It's essential to check the preferred route with each institution.

The academic calendar gives you extra time.
Because the academic year in Australia starts in February or March, UK students can apply after results day in August. Many courses also have a mid-year intake (usually July), which offers even more flexibility. For some students, this can be a good reason to take a short gap or work-based break while preparing to apply.

What is the ATAR?

The ATAR is a rank – not a score – that Australian universities use to compare applicants.

ATAR stands for Australian Tertiary Admission Rank. It ranges from 0 to 99.95 and shows a student's position relative to their national age group. An ATAR of 80, for example, means the student performed better than 80% of their peers.

As an international student, your qualifications will be converted into an ATAR equivalent.

When you apply with A levels or BTECs, the university or state admissions centre will assess your results and map them onto the ATAR system. Some universities publish clear ATAR-equivalent tables for international qualifications. Others assess each application individually.

You don't need to calculate this yourself – but you do need to check what ATAR equivalent your results are likely to produce. Each course has a minimum ATAR cut-off, which can change year by year.

A few examples:

- Competitive courses like Medicine or Law may require an ATAR of 90+.
- Most standard degree programmes will ask for an ATAR in the 70–85 range.
- TAFE-to-university pathways or foundation programmes may be open to students with lower results.

What advisers and teachers can do:

- Help students understand how their grades compare to ATAR equivalents.
- Use university websites or admissions guides to check typical entry cut-offs.
- Encourage realistic course selection based on predicted results, then refine post-results.
- Ensure students have a backup or insurance choice in case their actual grades are lower than predicted.
- Support students in providing official transcripts, certificates and any required English-language proof.

Case study: Tom – a vocational pathway through TAFE in Australia

Tom didn't want a traditional academic route – he wanted to learn by doing. In Year 12, he was studying for a mix of qualifications: BTEC Level 3 in engineering alongside an A level in maths. University didn't appeal to him at first, partly because he wasn't keen on writing essays or sitting more written exams. But when his college career adviser introduced him to the idea of studying in Australia through a TAFE (Technical and Further Education) programme, it clicked.

Tom researched TAFE colleges and focused on Queensland. He liked the look of TAFE Queensland, which offered a two-year Diploma of Engineering with the option to transfer into a university course later. The idea of building hands-on experience and then deciding whether to pursue a degree gave him breathing space. With help from his adviser, Tom applied directly through the TAFE website.

Entry requirements were achievable and BTECs were accepted. He didn't need to submit predicted grades – instead, TAFE asked for his completed BTEC results, evidence of English-language ability (his school certified English as his first language) and a statement about why he was interested in the course. Compared to UCAS, the application was more straightforward, with less emphasis on writing and more focus on his motivation and practical skills.

Tom started his course in February, six months after most of his friends began university in the UK. He used the time between results day and departure to work part-time and save money. On arrival, he moved into shared accommodation near campus and quickly got into the rhythm of practical, workshop-based learning. His course covered everything from computer-aided design (CAD) to electrical systems and safety protocols.

Life at TAFE: Practical, social and industry-focused

The atmosphere was different from school – more like a workplace. Tom's tutors were engineers themselves, and lessons focused on what employers actually expect on the job. Assessment was mostly project-based, with lots of teamwork and problem-solving. The class included local Australian students and international students from across Southeast Asia.

Outside of study, Tom joined a local football club and began part-time work. Australia allows international students to work up to 48 hours per fortnight during term, and Tom used that to pick up casual shifts in a hardware store. He appreciated the independence – financially and socially – and enjoyed the outdoor lifestyle and friendly pace of life in Brisbane.

At the end of his diploma, Tom had two options: get a job or move into university. He chose to apply to a partner university to complete a Bachelor of Engineering, entering straight into the second year. His TAFE grades, plus a recommendation from his tutor, made the process smooth.

Adviser insights

- TAFE offers a credible, affordable alternative to traditional university for students with vocational strengths.
- BTEC students may find more acceptance in the Australian TAFE system than at some UK universities.
- Advisers can play a key role by helping students understand pathway routes and build confidence in applying outside standard academic routes.
- The post-results application model gives flexibility and space to plan, especially for students who need time to mature or re-engage with learning.

Technical and Further Education (TAFE) and who it suits best

TAFE could be an ideal option for those looking for a more practical, career-oriented qualification. If you're drawn to hands-on fields such as hospitality, the trades or early childhood education, TAFE offers a direct, relevant pathway. It also suits students with BTECs or a mix of qualifications who may need a more flexible entry point. With smaller class sizes and a more personalised learning environment, TAFE provides a supportive setting. Additionally, completing a diploma can serve as a stepping stone into university, offering further academic and career progression.

What advisers and parents can do:

- Help students explore TAFE providers in different Australian states.
- Check which TAFE courses lead into university programmes.
- Compare TAFE entry requirements with A level or BTEC results.
- Encourage students to consider job outcomes as well as academic progression.
- Support with budgeting – TAFE courses are often more affordable, but living costs still apply.

Caps on international students

In recent years, the Australian Government has begun placing limits on international student numbers in certain high-demand regions to manage infrastructure and housing pressures. While these quotas are mostly targeted at large urban universities, prospective applicants should check for any changes to availability or entry caps in their chosen state.

(Australian Strategy for International Education 2021–2030, Department of Education)
www.education.gov.au

A different timeline: Applying to study in Australia

Year 12 (autumn to spring)

1. Start researching Australian universities and TAFE options.
2. Check entry requirements for your qualifications and whether the course starts in February or July.
3. Plan to take any necessary English-language tests and begin gathering key documents, such as school transcripts and passport copies.

Year 13 (spring to summer)

1. Focus on final exams and aim to complete any outstanding tests or paperwork.
2. After results are released in August, begin the application directly to institutions or through the relevant state portal.
3. Submit official documents and meet any specific course requirements, such as interviews or portfolios.

Post-results (late summer to autumn)
1. Apply for a student visa.
2. Arrange accommodation, health insurance and flights.
3. Prepare for a February or July course start, depending on the intake you choose.

Key dates
- Main intake: February or March (applications typically submitted August–October).
- Alternative intake: July (applications often open February–April).

Studying in New Zealand: A smaller system, strong global presence

New Zealand offers a more intimate university landscape with high academic standards and a strong quality of life.
If you're looking for a globally recognised degree in an English-speaking country, New Zealand is a great option. The country has eight universities, all publicly funded and consistently ranked in the top 3% worldwide. Its small size means the system is easy to navigate, and international students often benefit from personalised support and accessible campuses.

Applications are made directly to each university.
There's no national system like UCAS. Instead, you apply directly through each institution's international admissions portal. Most universities offer rolling admissions, meaning you can apply at different points in the year – although early planning is still advised.

The academic calendar aligns closely with Australia.
New Zealand's university year starts in late February or early March, with a second intake in July for many programmes. Like Australia, most institutions require actual grades rather than predicted ones. This means UK students usually apply after receiving their results.

UK qualifications are widely accepted – but BTEC recognition can vary.
A levels are understood and accepted across all universities. BTECs may be accepted for some courses, particularly if paired with additional academic qualifications. Each university publishes entry guidance for UK qualifications, and some will consider applications case by case.

Living and studying in New Zealand offers more than just a degree.
Students are drawn by the lifestyle, safety and strong focus on wellbeing. The country's stunning natural environment is a bonus, but it also contributes to a culture that values balance and student welfare. New Zealand also allows international students to work part-time during term and apply for a post-study work visa after graduation.

What advisers and parents can do:
- Help students compare entry requirements and application timelines across the eight universities.

Study Abroad Made Simple

- Encourage direct contact with admissions offices where BTECs or mixed qualifications are involved.
- Support with logistics like visas and insurance – similar to Australia
- Consider lifestyle factors, including travel distance, cost of living and access to support.

Asia: High standards, varied systems

Asia offers some of the most competitive and academically rigorous university options in the world. If you're aiming high and ready for a challenge, universities in countries like Hong Kong, Singapore, Japan and South Korea could be worth considering. These institutions often appear in global rankings, especially in STEM fields, business and technology. However, entry requirements can be tough, and each country has its own rules.

No single application model: Every country is different

There's no UCAS-style system across Asia. Instead, each country – and sometimes each university – has its own admissions portal and process.

- **Hong Kong** has clear, UK-friendly options. Universities like HKU and CUHK accept A levels, with the application procedure similar to UCAS in some cases.
- **Singapore** offers places at highly ranked institutions like NUS and NTU. Applications are direct, and A levels are accepted – but offers are based on very high grades. Singapore offers places at top-ranked institutions such as NUS and NTU. These universities accept A levels, IB, and in some cases, SATs with APs or high school diplomas for international students, especially those outside the UK system. Admissions policies in Singapore reflect national efforts to attract high-achieving international students across a range of qualifications. SATs, APs and A levels are all accepted, but offers often align with the country's strategic goals – particularly in science, technology and business.

   (Ministry of Education Singapore – Admissions Guidelines for International Students, www.moe.gov.sg*)*

- **Japan** and **South Korea** often require additional entrance exams. Some courses are taught in English, but local language skills may be needed, particularly for student life and job opportunities. Japan and South Korea offer world-class universities, but their admissions systems are highly structured and exam-focused. Students applying to top institutions such as the University of Tokyo, Kyoto University or Seoul National University will usually need to submit strong A level results or recognised international qualifications such as the IB Diploma or SATs. However, many of these universities operate on a dual-track system: domestic applicants sit rigorous local entrance exams, while international applicants apply through a dedicated global admissions route.

7 Exploring the East: Applying to Asia, New Zealand and Australia

Considerations for Asia

Increasingly, universities in both Japan and South Korea offer English-taught degree programmes, especially in Business, Science and International Studies. These are designed to attract international students and often have separate admissions windows, course codes and documentation requirements. That said, applicants should be prepared to provide a personal statement, academic references, proof of English proficiency (IELTS/TOEFL) if English is not the student's first language, and in some cases, undertake university-set exams or interviews.

Language ability matters outside the classroom. While many degree programmes are in English, day-to-day life on campus and in accommodation may be conducted in Japanese or Korean. Universities often offer free or subsidised language courses to help international students settle in.

Admissions criteria vary by institution and change frequently, so students – and advisers – are encouraged to contact international admissions offices directly. These dedicated administrators employed by most institutions are very useful in helping applicants navigate the entire process.

(Sources: Japan Study Support – www.jpss.jp; *Study in Korea* – www.studyinkorea.go.kr)*

For students taking A levels, there are options across the region – but requirements are strict. For students taking BTECs, options are extremely limited. Most universities will not recognise vocational qualifications unless paired with other credentials like A levels, IB or SATs.

Entrance exams and academic testing

In many Asian systems, academic achievement is the main – and sometimes only – criterion for entry.

Some universities may ask for:

- SATs, APs or IB scores (especially in Japan, South Korea and Malaysia);
- English proficiency tests (IELTS or TOEFL);
- Local university entrance exams, which may include maths, writing or science papers.

If you're applying to a course taught in English, you may still be expected to prove your language level or take university-specific assessments. Sometimes an exemption letter provided by the school to certify that the student has English as their first language is sufficient.

Timing, documentation and logistics

Applications typically open earlier than in the UK – often in the autumn of Year 13, or even late Year 12. Deadlines vary, and because systems are decentralised, you'll need to keep track of each university's requirements. Many ask for:

- Final exam certificates and transcripts (translated if needed);
- A statement of purpose or essay (not the same as a UCAS personal statement);
- Recommendation letters from up to three teachers or advisers;
- Evidence of financial support or visa eligibility.

What advisers and parents can do:

- Help students identify which Asian countries offer courses in English.
- Encourage early planning – ideally starting in Year 11 or 12.
- Support students through documentation and translation requirements.
- Advise realistically about academic expectations and potential culture shock.
- Explore whether a foundation year or international pathway programme may offer a smoother entry route.

Language requirements and cultural fit

English is widely used in higher education across Asia – but it's not always the only language you'll need.

Many universities in countries like Hong Kong, Singapore and Malaysia offer entire degree programmes taught in English. These are designed for both local and international students. In contrast, institutions in Japan, South Korea and China may offer English-medium courses, but much of campus life – from admin to accommodation – may still operate in the local language.

Language requirements vary – and may affect more than just the classroom.

Even if your course is taught in English, you'll likely be asked to prove your proficiency with an IELTS or TOEFL score. Some universities set minimum scores for both overall achievement and individual skills like writing or speaking.

If you plan to study in a non-English-speaking country, think about your comfort level. Everyday tasks like shopping, travel and joining clubs may involve the local language. While this can be exciting, it can also be isolating without preparation.

Case study: Lily — choosing Hong Kong for a creative degree

Lily was born and raised in the UK, but her family roots are in Hong Kong. By the time she reached Year 12, she was seriously considering studying abroad. She was drawn to Hong Kong for its creative energy, international outlook and personal significance – her parents had both grown up there. She decided to apply to a university in HK to study Art.

She was studying A levels in English, geography and art. With predicted grades of AAB, Lily applied to the University of Hong Kong (HKU) as her first choice and City University of Hong Kong (CityU) as her insurance. Both institutions offered strong art and design programmes, but HKU was the more academically competitive of the two.

Alongside her application, Lily prepared and submitted a portfolio of her work. This was a key part of the admissions process, and she dedicated a lot of time in the spring term to developing and curating it. Her school helped her gather transcripts, references and predicted grades – although the process was more manual and less familiar than UCAS.

When results day came, Lily achieved ABB: one grade lower than predicted in Art. Because Art was her intended degree subject, HKU withdrew their offer, having required at least an A. Fortunately, Lily had met the conditions for CityU, which accepted her without delay. She confirmed her place and started planning her move.

Life in Hong Kong as an international student

Adjusting to university life in Hong Kong was challenging at first – but energising.

Lily arrived a few weeks before term started and moved into university accommodation. The pace of the city was intense, and the heat and humidity took getting used to, but she was excited by how much there was to see and do. Her campus was modern, with excellent digital design facilities, and she quickly connected with other international students from across Asia, Europe and North America.

The teaching style was a mix of lectures, studio sessions and independent projects. In her first semester, Lily worked on multimedia pieces and experimental installations, and was encouraged to take creative risks. While there was a strong focus on practical outcomes, the course also explored art history and theory with an Asian perspective – something Lily hadn't encountered much in the UK.

Outside of class, the city became part of her education. Hong Kong's galleries, street art and design culture provided endless inspiration. Lily often took the MTR to explore exhibitions and markets after class. She also reconnected with extended family, who helped her settle in and understand local customs. While English was widely spoken at university, she found that learning a few basic Cantonese phrases helped her feel more at home.

By the end of her first year, Lily had built a creative portfolio and a new sense of independence.

Although missing out on HKU had been disappointing, CityU proved a better fit for her artistic development. She now plans to stay in Hong Kong after graduation to work in the local design industry.

Adviser reflections

- Students with A levels are often well positioned for entry into Hong Kong's top universities – but final grades matter.
- For portfolio-based subjects, performance in the relevant subject (e.g. art) carries extra weight.

- Hong Kong offers a strong mix of academic depth and creative opportunity, especially in fields like design and media.
- Advisers can support students by encouraging early portfolio preparation, managing expectations around predicted v. actual grades, and helping with cultural and practical planning.

Admission to Hong Kong's publicly funded universities is highly competitive. Institutions are restricted by policy to offering no more than 20% of their undergraduate places to international students – a category that includes UK applicants, even those with family connections to the region.

(University Grants Committee, Hong Kong SAR)

www.ugc.edu.hk

How do the systems compare?

Table 7.1 provides a quick overview of how university applications work in Australia, New Zealand and Asia. It summarises timelines, entry requirements, qualification

TABLE 7.1 Asia and Australasia compared

Feature	Australia	New Zealand	Asia
Application route	State-based portals (e.g. UAC, VTAC) or direct to institution.	Direct to institution.	Mostly direct to institution; some national platforms (e.g. Hong Kong's JUPAS for local students).
Academic year starts	February/March (main); July (some courses).	February/March (main); July (some courses).	Varies widely – often August/September; some have spring and autumn intakes.
Predicted grades accepted?	Usually not – requires actual grades.	Usually not – actual grades required.	Rarely – most expect final results or international qualifications already completed such as SAT.
A levels accepted?	Yes	Yes	Varies – more common in Hong Kong and Singapore; less so elsewhere.
BTECs accepted?	Partially – depends on course and university.	Sometimes – case by case.	Rarely – generally not accepted without additional qualifications.
Entry requirements format	Converted to ATAR equivalent.	Converted to NCEA or assessed individually.	Varies – may require entrance tests, SATs, APs or local equivalents.
English-language requirements	Yes – IELTS/TOEFL for most.	Yes – similar to Australia.	Yes – some courses require local language too.
Post-study work visas available?	Yes – generous options for international graduates.	Yes – one to three years depending on level.	Some countries offer this, but not guaranteed.
Lifestyle benefits	High quality of life, large international student population.	Safe, scenic, supportive environment.	Rich cultural exposure, career potential, but language/cultural adaptation required.

recognition and practical considerations. Advisers can use it to help make informed decisions about where to apply – and advisers will find it a useful tool for guiding conversations with families considering international routes.

Final word

Studying in Asia or Australia is not just an academic choice – it's a personal journey. Whether your students are aiming for a globally ranked university, a creative programme like Lily's or a vocational route like Tom's, the key is early, informed planning. There are many routes to success – and each one starts with knowing what fits you best.

Adviser checklist

When guiding a student who is considering study in Asia or Australasia, work through the steps below to ensure they choose the right route, understand the requirements and meet all deadlines.

Establish the student's starting point
- [x] Confirm predicted or actual results.
- [x] Note whether they are taking A levels, BTECs, IB or a combination.
- [x] Check if their qualifications meet entry requirements for the destination country.

Match qualifications to the target system
- [x] Recognise that A levels are widely accepted in Australia, New Zealand, Hong Kong and Singapore.
- [x] Be aware that BTECs often have greater recognition in Australia and New Zealand than in much of Asia; where accepted in Asia, they are usually combined with A levels or an IB diploma.
- [x] Some Asian universities (including in Singapore and Japan) accept SATs or IB in place of A levels.

Plan for application timing
- [x] Note that most Asian universities require actual grades, not predicted ones.
- [x] Remember that Australia and New Zealand's academic year begins in February or March, with some courses starting in July.
- [x] Support the student in planning applications after results day, allowing time for visa processing and travel arrangements.

Explore all suitable routes
- [x] Consider TAFE colleges in Australia for students seeking hands-on, job-ready qualifications, with potential progression to university.

- ☑ Recommend foundation years or pathway programmes if the student's qualifications are not directly recognised.
- ☑ For portfolio-based courses (such as Art or Design), check additional requirements and earlier deadlines.

Address cultural and practical readiness
- ☑ Verify the language of instruction, support services and visa conditions.
- ☑ Discuss the student's readiness to live far from home – financially, emotionally and socially.
- ☑ Facilitate connections with students who have already studied abroad, and encourage research into both academic and daily life abroad.

Ongoing adviser support
- ☑ Encourage early research in Year 11 or Year 12, especially for portfolio or test-based courses.
- ☑ Help students assess academic fit realistically and plan for flexibility.
- ☑ Promote backup choices and confirm recognition of all qualifications, including BTECs.
- ☑ Stay involved with logistics: document preparation, English-language testing and monitoring of application timelines.

FURTHER INFORMATION

If your students are thinking about applying to a university or college in Asia or Australia, the following resources can help you take the next steps. Use them to explore entry requirements, course options and application timelines – and don't be afraid to contact institutions directly if you're unsure.

Asia

Study in Hong Kong: Official site offering application guidance, course information and scholarship opportunities for international students.
www.studyinhongkong.edu.hk

Ministry of Education, Singapore: Admissions Guidelines for International Students: Comprehensive guide to applying to Singaporean universities, including entry requirements and accepted qualifications.
www.moe.gov.sg

Japan Study Support (JPSS): Detailed listings of English-taught programmes, entry requirements and support services for studying in Japan.
www.jpss.jp

Study in Korea: Government-supported site for prospective students interested in Korean universities, including admissions processes and visa information.
www.studyinkorea.go.kr

QS Top Universities: Study in Asia: Searchable database and articles covering institutions across Asia, with advice on rankings, scholarships and student life.
www.topuniversities.com/where-to-study/asia

Australia

Study Australia: Official Australian Government guide for international students.
www.studyaustralia.gov.au

TAFE Queensland – Example of a large TAFE provider with diploma and pathway programmes.
www.tafeqld.edu.au

University Admissions Centres – Use these to apply to universities in each state:

  UAC (NSW/ACT) – www.uac.edu.au
  VTAC (Victoria) – www.vtac.edu.au
  QTAC (Queensland) – www.qtac.edu.au

New Zealand

Study With New Zealand – Government-backed site covering all universities and visas.
www.studywithnewzealand.govt.nz

8 Transatlantic aspirations: Applying to the US and Canada

This chapter will:

- Compare the academic, cultural and personal advantages of studying in the USA or Canada, including liberal arts degrees, co-op placements and the concept of institutional 'fit'.
- Demystify the application process, from Common App and UC to OUAC, highlighting how it differs from the UK system.
- Break down holistic admissions, including personal essays, references and extracurriculars, with tips on helping students craft authentic narratives.
- Explain how UK qualifications convert into North American standards, covering transcripts, GPA and standardised tests such as the SAT and ACT.
- Outline tuition costs and financial aid differ from the rest of the world, with tailored advice for UK applicants, including Ivy League expectations and translating terminology.

Why study in the US or Canada?

Many students think about the US and Canada together when weighing up North American study options. Although each country has its own rules and quirks, both share a broadly holistic admissions philosophy that to a greater extent looks beyond just exam results – bringing in personal essays, extracurricular activities, multiple references and wider context, which sets them apart from other countries. Because this approach cuts across both systems, it makes sense to thread them together here, rather than split them rigidly, as has been the approach in previous chapters. The following section highlights how their processes overlap and where they differ, so you can compare your options clearly without reading the same advice twice.

Studying in North America offers UK students a unique opportunity to combine academic rigour with a broader educational experience. With world-class universities, diverse course options and vibrant campus cultures, both the US and Canada present exciting alternatives to traditional UK routes.

8 Transatlantic aspirations: applying to the US and Canada

Flexibility and choice

Unlike the UK system, most American universities – and many Canadian ones – allow students to explore several subjects before committing to a major. This is ideal for students with wide interests or those still deciding on a direction, with most undergraduate bachelor courses being four years in duration.

Prestigious institutions

From Ivy League universities to top-ranking Canadian institutions like McGill and the University of Toronto, both countries offer internationally recognised qualifications that can open doors worldwide.

Campus life

Universities in the US and Canada offer rich extracurricular options, from research and student societies to sport and community engagement. Students are encouraged to get involved and develop skills outside the classroom.

Strong career outcomes

Graduates are highly employable, benefiting from an education that fosters critical thinking, communication and adaptability. Many Canadian universities also offer co-op programmes, combining academic study with paid work placements.

A global perspective

Beyond academics, studying abroad fosters independence, resilience and a global outlook – qualities that serve students well long after graduation.

Case study: Chris — from California to a career in computing

Chris, a student with a strong academic foundation and a clear passion for technology, chose to pursue his undergraduate studies in the US. He was accepted into the University of California, Santa Barbara (UCSB), where he completed a bachelor's in Computer Science, before progressing to a master's degree at UCLA (University of California, Los Angeles).

Chris's application stood out thanks to his excellent standardised test scores: an SAT score of 1510, a TOEFL score of 114 (used to demonstrate English proficiency), and an outstanding GRE score of 333. The GRE (Graduate Record Examination) is commonly required for entry into US postgraduate programmes. It assesses verbal reasoning, quantitative reasoning and analytical writing. With a maximum combined score of 340, Chris's result placed him in the top few percent of test-takers globally – reflecting advanced skills in both critical thinking and numerical analysis. He had also published two academic papers, further demonstrating his readiness for graduate-level study. His extracurricular activities reinforced a well-rounded profile.

> Reflecting on his experience, Chris describes his time in California as 'enriching'. He highlights the open academic culture, which encouraged creativity, freedom of thought and active discussion – something he found distinct from his earlier educational experiences. 'I was exposed to a new academic environment that encouraged open discussion, creativity and freedom', he says. 'I got to see new artworks, experience new cultures, and meet people from all over the world.'
>
> While Chris is quick to recommend the experience to others, he also shares some of the challenges he encountered. 'Being away from home can be difficult,' he admits. 'There were times when I felt homesick, and accessing healthcare and dealing with visa logistics was sometimes stressful.'
>
> Despite these occasional hurdles, Chris believes his decision to study in the US was transformative; he had a strong desire for a change of scenery, and he was fortunate enough that his parents were willing and able to support him financially. Ultimately, he wanted to build a life in the US. His time at UCSB and UCLA not only broadened his academic horizons but also shaped his confidence, independence and supported his long-term career ambitions.

Key differences from the UK application process

Applying to universities in the US and Canada presents a distinct set of procedures compared to the UK's UCAS system. Understanding these differences is crucial for UK students considering transatlantic study.

Decentralised application systems

In the UK, UCAS serves as a centralised platform for university applications. Conversely, the US and Canada employ decentralised systems, although the level of centralisation is increasing all the time:

- **US**: The Common Application (Common App) is widely used, allowing students to apply to multiple institutions through a single platform. However, many universities also require supplemental essays or additional materials specific to their institution. The University Colleges (UCs), based in California, also have their own portal.
- **Canada**: Application processes vary by province and institution. For example, Ontario universities use the Ontario Universities' Application Centre (OUAC), while other provinces may have their own systems or require direct applications to individual universities.

Holistic admissions approach

US and Canadian universities often adopt a holistic admissions process, assessing applicants beyond academic achievements. This includes evaluating personal essays, extracurricular involvement, letters of recommendation and, in some cases, interviews. This contrasts with the UK system, which primarily focuses on academic performance and predicted grades. The mindset of admissions tutors is entirely different – something UK advisers must be mindful of, as it is a very different philosophy.

Varied deadlines and admission plans

Application timelines in North America differ significantly:

US

Institutions may offer Early Action, Early Decision, Regular Decision or Rolling Admissions, each with its own deadlines and implications for applicants.

Early Action (EA) allows students to apply to their chosen universities earlier than the standard deadline – typically by 1 November or 15 November for US institutions. Applicants receive a decision well in advance, usually by mid-December, but unlike Early Decision, EA is *non-binding*. This means students can apply to other institutions and are not required to accept an offer immediately.

Early Decision (ED) is also an early application process, with deadlines generally falling around 1 November. However, ED is *binding*, which means if a student is accepted, they must attend that institution and withdraw any other applications. It is suitable for applicants who are certain about their first-choice university. Some universities also offer ED II, with a later deadline in early January, providing a second chance to apply under binding conditions.

With binding applications, students and advisers are required to sign a declaration on submission which legally binds them to the institution.

The Regular Decision (RD) route is the most common and flexible. Deadlines typically fall between 1 January and 15 January (for US universities), with decisions released by March or April. This pathway is non-binding, giving applicants time to compare offers and financial aid packages before committing.

Rolling Admissions. In a Rolling Admissions system, applications are reviewed as they are received, and decisions are made on a continuous basis – often within four to six weeks of submission. There is no fixed deadline, though it is advisable to apply early, as spaces may fill up quickly. Rolling Admissions is common among US institutions for certain foundation and degree programmes, as well as some international universities.

Canada

Deadlines vary by province and institution. It's common for applications to be submitted 8 to 12 months before the intended start date.

Understanding these timelines is essential to ensure timely submission of applications and supporting documents.

Emphasis on personal narrative

Personal essays play a pivotal role in North American applications. Unlike the UK personal statement, which focuses on academic interests and achievements, US and Canadian essays often explore personal experiences, challenges overcome and individual growth. Crafting a compelling narrative that reflects the applicant's character and aspirations is vital as institutions are concerned, perhaps more than anywhere else in the world, that the student is the 'right fit'.

Letters of recommendation

Letters of recommendation are a standard requirement in US and Canadian applications. Students should seek references from teachers, mentors or workplace supervisors who can provide detailed insights into their academic abilities, character and potential contributions to the university community.

Transcripts and grading systems

Applicants must provide transcripts detailing their academic performance. Understanding how UK qualifications translate into the North American grading context is important. For instance, A level results may be evaluated differently, and some institutions may require additional documentation to assess equivalency.

Understanding US and Canadian terminology

One of the first challenges UK students face when applying to universities in North America is the unfamiliar terminology. The educational landscape in the US and Canada is shaped by different systems, values and structures – and this is reflected in the language they use.

Whether you're reading course descriptions, submitting documents or speaking with admissions staff, understanding the key terms is essential. This section decodes the most important concepts and explains how they relate to the UK context.

Academic terminology and structures

- **Transcript**
  A transcript is a complete record of your academic achievement, usually including individual subjects, marks and qualifications. UK students typically provide a transcript with their GCSE and A level results, as well as predicted grades if still studying. Some US and Canadian universities may also request *mid-year* or *term reports* from your school, depending on when you apply. These reports give universities a sense of your academic trajectory and work ethic.

- **Grade Point Average (GPA)**
  While the UK uses letter grades and percentage marks, most US and some Canadian universities evaluate academic performance using GPA – a scale usually ranging from 0 to 4.0. You won't typically be asked to convert your UK grades yourself, but understanding this scale can help you interpret entry requirements or compare your standing to local applicants. Universities accustomed to international applicants will interpret your qualifications appropriately, and some may use credential evaluation services.

- **Major and Minor**
  These terms define the structure of a US undergraduate degree. A *major* is your primary field of study – roughly equivalent to your course subject in the UK – while a *minor* is a secondary area that complements or contrasts with it. It's common for students to take time to choose a major, and most declare it in their second year. This flexibility is a key feature of the liberal arts model. In Canada, degrees may also offer majors and minors, but the path is usually more structured, similar to the UK.

- **Liberal arts and general education**
  In the US, particularly at smaller colleges, students often follow a liberal arts curriculum. This approach encourages broad learning across the humanities, sciences and social sciences before specialisation. Even at research universities, students may be required to complete general education modules, such as writing or quantitative reasoning, regardless of their intended major.

- **Freshman, sophomore, junior, senior**
  These refer to the four undergraduate years in the US:
  - *Freshman* (first year);
  - *Sophomore* (second year);
  - *Junior* (third year);
  - *Senior* (final year).

  In Canada, students are usually referred to by their year (e.g. 'first-year student') rather than these labels, but US-style terminology may still appear.

- **Community college and transfers**
  Community colleges in the US offer two-year associate degrees and often serve as stepping stones to four-year institutions. Students can 'transfer' to complete a bachelor's degree, and this can be a more affordable path to a top university. Some Canadian colleges also operate a similar transfer model.

- **Co-op (Co-operative education)**
  Especially prominent in Canada, co-op programmes combine academic study with structured, paid work experience. These are built into the degree and offer students a chance to graduate with a strong CV and professional contacts, comparable to 'sandwich courses' in the UK.

Admissions-specific language

- **Common App Essay versus Personal Statement**
  The Common App essay is the US equivalent of the UK personal statement – but with a different tone and purpose. Rather than focusing on academic interest, it invites applicants to share a personal story or insight that reveals something about their character. It's more narrative in style and can draw on personal experiences, challenges or moments of growth. Students should expect to write multiple essays, including supplementary essays for individual universities.

- **SAT/ACT**
  These standardised tests are unique to the US and used by many universities as part of the application process. However, the *test-optional* movement has grown significantly in recent years, and many institutions no longer require them. Canadian universities rarely require SAT or ACT scores, especially for UK applicants.

Language and cultural nuances

It's not just terminology that differs – tone and style matter too. In North America, students are encouraged to be self-reflective and confident, especially in essays and interviews. Describing your strengths or sharing a story of personal development is not seen as boastful, but as part of showing who you are. This can feel unfamiliar to UK students used to more modest, understated approaches.

Key components of the application

Applying to North American universities involves more than submitting grades. The application process is holistic, meaning universities want to understand who you are beyond your academic record. Each part of the application plays a role in painting that broader picture.

Academic transcripts

Your transcript is the academic heart of your application. For UK students, this typically includes:

- GCSE and Year 10 results;
- AS level (or equivalent) results and predicted grades for remaining qualifications;
- Any relevant internal assessments or teacher comments.

Your school may need to compile this into a single document, especially if your qualifications are still in progress. Some institutions, particularly in the US, also request a mid-year report from your teachers during your final year. It is also a requirement to include 4 years' worth of grades, which means for US applicants the school will need to look back on end-of-term grades from Year 10 (first year of KS4). Typically, transcripts also require a GPA, but the Common App questions on submission allow a centre to state that 'GPA is not normally calculated', so as to not disadvantage the candidate by not including it.

In Canada, universities may make conditional offers based on predicted grades, though requirements vary by province and institution. Be sure your school is familiar with the format and deadlines required by each university.

Personal essay or statement

In the US, the Common App essay is a key feature. It differs from the UK personal statement in tone and purpose. Rather than focusing on subject interest and course suitability, the Common App essay is more personal. It might explore a formative life experience, a challenge you've overcome or a moment that shaped your worldview. The aim is to reveal your character, values and potential as a university community member.

On top of the main essay, many US universities require supplemental essays that address topics like: why do you want to attend this institution? How will you contribute to our campus community? Describe an activity that's meaningful to you.

Canadian universities rarely require personal essays, but some competitive programmes – particularly in business, engineering or scholarships – may request a statement of interest or similar.

Letters of recommendation

Most North American institutions request two to three references. These should come from teachers who know the student well and can speak to their academic strengths, classroom behaviour and potential. You may also be asked for a school counsellor reference – if your school doesn't have one, a head of sixth form or form tutor can often write this instead.

Tip: Choose referees who can offer specific examples of your contributions, growth or leadership. A vague or overly general letter is less impactful than one that provides vivid detail. The Head of Year letter should be written after interviewing the student to gain as much insight as possible and ensure it complements the essay.

Standardised tests: SAT and ACT

Some US universities still require SAT or ACT scores, though many have moved to test-optional policies. This means you can choose whether or not to submit test scores, and doing so won't harm your chances if you opt out – provided your academic record is strong.

If you do decide to take a test:

- SAT focuses on evidence-based reading, writing and maths;
- ACT includes English, maths, reading, science and an optional essay.

The ACT and SAT are both standardised tests used in university admissions in the US, but they have distinct origins and formats that reflect different educational priorities.

The SAT (Scholastic Assessment Test) was introduced in the 1920s by the College Board. It was designed as an aptitude test to assess a student's reasoning and problem-solving skills, aiming to offer a more level playing field in university admissions regardless of a student's educational background. Over time, it has evolved to place greater emphasis on academic skills, particularly in evidence-based reading, writing and mathematics.

In contrast, the ACT (American College Test), launched in 1959, was developed as an achievement test to better reflect what students had learnt in school. It was created in response to concerns that the SAT didn't accurately measure classroom learning. The ACT includes four core sections – English, Maths, Reading and Science – plus an optional writing component, and it tends to appeal to students who perform well in school-based assessments.

In essence, while both tests now serve a similar purpose and are accepted interchangeably by most universities, the SAT traditionally focused on innate aptitude, whereas the ACT was rooted in curriculum-based knowledge. Their continued use today reflects the diversity in student learning styles and the flexibility institutions seek in understanding academic potential. They were developed to provide a level playing field for admissions, given that, unlike the UK, the US does not have a national curriculum prescribed by the central government. More information on scoring and preparation for these assessments can be found in Chapter 5.

Canadian universities generally do not require these tests for UK applicants with A levels.

Extracurricular activities

This is where you can really stand out. US universities place strong emphasis on what you do outside the classroom – sports, music, volunteering, part-time work, clubs, personal projects or leadership roles all count. The Common App allows space to list up to ten activities, ranked by importance and time commitment.

Canadian universities may not require a formal list of extracurriculars unless applying for a specific programme or scholarship, but including these achievements in your application can still be valuable.

Application fees and waivers

Most North American institutions charge an application fee – typically between £50–£100 per application. Fee waivers are available for students from lower-income backgrounds. If this applies to your student, check each university's financial support pages for advice.

Supporting applicants with the essay process

For many UK students, writing a university essay for an American or Canadian application can feel unfamiliar. Unlike the UCAS personal statement, these essays focus less on academic readiness for a specific course and more on character, voice and potential.

The main essay, usually submitted through the Common App or a similar platform, gives students the chance to reflect on their values, experiences and ambitions in a more personal, conversational style. Advisers should reassure students that authenticity and thoughtful reflection matter far more than polished perfection.

For detailed guidance on choosing topics, structuring an essay and maintaining a clear, personal voice, see *Guiding students through the US college essay* in Chapter 4.

In addition to the main essay, many applicants will also write shorter supplementary responses. These often have tight word counts and deadlines, so encourage students to plan ahead, draft early and seek honest feedback from trusted readers.

Advisers play an important role in managing timelines, guiding self-reflection without over-editing and reminding students that small, specific moments can be just as powerful as dramatic stories. The aim is to help each student stay confident and genuine, whether they are developing ideas, sharing drafts with peers or polishing a final version.

Clear guidance and realistic support help students keep the writing truly their own and resist the temptation to rely too heavily on AI shortcuts.

UK-US vocabulary watchpoints

Help students watch out for regional language. For example:

- 'Mum' → 'Mom' (if writing for a US audience – or use a neutral term like 'my mother').
- 'College' in the UK often refers to sixth-form or FE institutions, but in the US it means university.
- Avoid UK-specific educational terms unless explained (e.g. A levels, sixth form).

Finding the right fit

In the US and Canada, students are encouraged to think not just about where they can *get in*, but where they will *fit in*. It's a key cultural difference from the UK system, where course content and entry requirements often dominate decision-making. In North America, the concept of 'fit' combines academic, personal and social considerations – and it's central to how institutions present themselves and how they select applicants.

Liberal arts colleges v. large universities

In the US especially, students can choose between:

- **Liberal arts colleges**, which are usually smaller, undergraduate-focused institutions that encourage broad learning and close student–faculty interaction.
- **Research universities**, which are larger, with a wider range of courses, more postgraduates and an emphasis on academic research.

Both have their merits. Liberal arts colleges may offer more personal attention and flexibility, while larger universities might provide a greater variety of programmes, facilities and global name recognition.

In Canada, most institutions are public research universities, though they still vary widely in culture, size and specialisms.

What do you want from your degree?

When considering university options, students should reflect on what kind of environment will allow them to thrive. Some may wish to explore a range of subjects before narrowing their academic focus, making broader liberal arts models particularly appealing. Others might have a clear direction already and prefer a more specialised programme.

The learning environment is equally important. Would they feel more at ease in small, discussion-based classes, or are they comfortable in large lecture halls with hundreds of students? The physical setting matters too – some students are energised by being close to a major city, while others prefer the intimacy and community of a self-contained campus.

It's also worth thinking about the kind of student body they want to be part of. Would they feel most at home among peers who are academically driven, creatively inclined, socially active, sporty or from diverse international backgrounds? There's no single right answer, but taking time to consider these preferences can lead to better decisions and greater personal fulfilment.

While academic reputation and course content matter, students' university choices are often shaped just as much by personal and social factors. Research by Hossler, Schmit and Vesper (1999) shows that influences such as parental expectations, peer opinion and perceptions of campus culture play a major role in decision-making. This underlines the importance of considering not just where a student can get in, but where they are likely to feel comfortable, supported and motivated to succeed.

This is particularly important in North America, where your *campus experience* is often just as important as your academic one.

Making use of resources

There are several ways students can research fit:

- University websites – especially student blogs, virtual tours and video content;
- Admissions webinars and virtual Q&As;
- Social media – many institutions post student takeovers or campus events;
- Online tools – platforms like BigFuture (College Board), Unigo or Times Higher Education rankings with filters by student life and support services;
- Speaking to alumni – if your school has former students at North American universities, encourage applicants to get in touch.

Trusting your instincts

Fit is not always something you can measure. Sometimes, a student connects with a particular university's values, traditions or way of teaching. Encourage them to listen to that instinct – and remind them that being in the 'right' place for them is far more powerful than chasing a big name that doesn't suit their needs. Wherever feasible, students should visit the campus in advance to get a genuine sense of the environment and culture.

Costs and funding

Studying in the US or Canada can be a transformative experience – but it often comes at a higher cost than studying in the UK. That said, a wide range of financial aid and scholarship options exist, and many UK students do succeed in securing significant support. Chapter 10 outlines these issues in detail, but the following section deals with financial aspects particular to the US and Canada.

Understanding tuition, living costs and available funding is a crucial step in making a confident, informed decision.

Tuition fees: A wide range

Unlike UK universities, where tuition fees are broadly standardised, fees in North America vary significantly between institutions:

- **US**:
  Tuition at private universities can range from $30,000 to $60,000 per year (approx. £24,000–£48,000), while public (state) universities typically charge international students between $20,000 and $40,000 (£16,000–£32,000).
- **Canada**:
  Fees for international students tend to be lower than in the US, generally falling between CAD$20,000–CAD$40,000 (£12,000–£24,000) per year, depending on the institution and programme.

Living costs also vary: urban campuses like New York or Toronto will typically be more expensive than rural or small-town settings.

In Canada, some provinces or national schemes also provide support to international students with exceptional promise.

Budgeting and planning ahead

Start early. Many scholarships have autumn deadlines, often well before application closing dates. Encourage students to:

- Research costs early and build a rough budget.
- Identify possible sources of funding – from universities and external providers.
- Keep a clear calendar of application deadlines.
- Seek help with any forms – some aid forms can be complex and time-consuming (e.g. the CSS Profile required by some US universities).

While a full breakdown of funding options, visas and work rules is covered in Chapter 10, it's helpful to include some key points here to highlight how costs and financial aid can differ between the US and Canada. Many families consider these practical details alongside admissions requirements when deciding which North American route is the best fit.

A note on value

Finally, remind students that cost doesn't always equate to value. Some of the most expensive universities also offer the most generous financial aid. And for students who make use of everything North American universities offer – from academic challenge to career preparation – the investment can pay lifelong dividends.

Spotlight: Applying to the Ivy League

For many UK students, the term *Ivy League* conjures images of ancient libraries, elite traditions and extraordinary academic reputations. Comprising eight highly selective universities in the north-eastern US, the Ivy League is admired worldwide – but also widely misunderstood.

This section explores what sets these institutions apart, who they're looking for and how UK students can approach the process with clarity and confidence.

What is the Ivy League?

Originally an athletics conference, the Ivy League now refers to: Harvard University, Yale University, Princeton University, Columbia University, Brown University, Dartmouth College University of Pennsylvania, Cornell University.

These are private, research-intensive universities with long histories, large endowments and highly competitive admissions. But they are far from identical – each has its own ethos, academic culture and student body. For example, Brown is known for its open curriculum, while Princeton emphasises undergraduate teaching and independent research.

What makes Ivy League admissions different?

They are not simply looking for the 'top' students on paper – they are looking for future leaders, original thinkers and contributors to their communities. Applicants must be exceptional.

Ivy League universities practise holistic admissions, meaning they evaluate applicants within the context of their personal, academic and social backgrounds. While academic excellence is essential, these institutions are not simply looking for the students with the highest grades or test scores. Instead, they seek individuals who demonstrate originality, leadership and the potential to make meaningful contributions to their university community and beyond.

Applicants are assessed on a broad range of qualities. Personal essays offer insight into a student's voice, values and motivation. Extracurricular involvement and leadership roles highlight commitment, curiosity and initiative. Strong letters of recommendation provide further context about a candidate's character and impact. Admissions teams also take into account family or school circumstances that may have shaped the student's journey, allowing a fairer view of potential.

In short, Ivy League admissions are about more than just numbers. They are about identifying future leaders – young people who are not only academically accomplished, but also thoughtful, resilient and driven to make a difference.

Academic expectations

Applicants from the UK are expected to be performing at the top of their year group. This typically includes:

- Outstanding GCSEs (or equivalent);
- Predicted grades of A*AA or above at A level (or 38+ in the IB);
- High achievement in relevant subjects;
- Strong performance in any standardised tests (if submitted).

Some Ivy League schools, such as Yale and Princeton, are test-optional, meaning applicants are not required to submit SAT or ACT scores. However, submitting strong scores can still be helpful – particularly for international applicants.

Essays that show depth and personality

Each Ivy League institution sets its own essay prompts – and takes them seriously. These may include:

- Reflections on your intellectual interests.
- Descriptions of a community you belong to.
- Insights into your values, identity or aspirations.

Essays are a chance to show more than academic ability. The most compelling ones are personal, reflective and specific. They reveal how you think, what matters to you and what kind of classmate you'll be.

Encourage students to avoid the trap of writing what they *think* admissions officers want to hear. Authenticity is more memorable than perfection.

Standout extracurriculars

There's no single 'correct' activity. What Ivy League universities want to see is:

- Passion sustained over time;
- Leadership or initiative;

- Impact (in school, community, or wider world);
- Originality or entrepreneurial spirit.

A student doesn't need to have founded a charity or won a national award – but they do need to show genuine commitment, creativity and follow-through.

Letters of recommendation

These should come from teachers who know the student well and can speak to their curiosity, work ethic and classroom presence. Generic letters won't stand out – the best references are vivid and specific, offering insight into how a student learns and collaborates.

Financial aid and access

Most Ivy League universities offer need-blind admissions for US students and need-aware for international students – but all commit to meeting full demonstrated financial need. In some cases, UK applicants pay little or nothing if their family income falls below a certain threshold.

This makes Ivy League universities more financially accessible than many students expect. Applying may feel bold, but it's not out of reach.

Busting the myths
- You don't need to be a genius or a millionaire.
- You *can* apply from a state school and succeed.
- You don't need to have 'perfect' everything – what matters is fit, growth and potential.

The Ivy League isn't for everyone, and it shouldn't be the only goal – but for the right student, it can be an extraordinary opportunity. The key is to research each university individually, approach the process thoughtfully and apply with a sense of confidence and self-awareness.

Top tips for UK applicants

Applying to a university in the US or Canada can feel like stepping into a new world – and in some ways, it is. The systems, expectations and culture are different, but so are the opportunities. As a UK applicant, you bring a strong academic foundation and a distinctive educational perspective – now it's about learning how to present that in a way North American admissions teams will understand and value.

Here are some top tips to help UK students stand out and feel confident throughout the process.

1. Understand the systems early

The UK and Canadian admissions processes are multilayered and differ by institution. There's no single portal like UCAS, and deadlines can vary significantly – some as early as November for Early Decision. Start researching in Year 12 or earlier, and keep a clear record of each university's requirements.

2. Translate your education clearly

Admissions staff may not be familiar with the finer points of A levels, EPQs or BTECs. Use your transcript, references and essays to explain what you've studied and how your qualifications align with their expectations. If possible, include predicted grades and subject breakdowns.

For example:

- A level – equivalent to advanced placement (AP) courses in the US.
- EPQ – similar to a senior thesis or extended essay.

3. Use your personal essay strategically

Your UCAS personal statement won't serve the same purpose in a US or Canadian application. Instead, treat the Common App or supplemental essays as an opportunity to reflect on *who you are* – not just what you study. Think narrative, not academic CV. Be specific, be personal and be reflective.

4. Choose the right referees

Strong letters of recommendation can make a real difference. Choose teachers who know you well and can describe your work habits, curiosity and growth. Ask them early and provide context about what the university is looking for, so they can tailor their reference effectively.

5. Be confident but sincere

North American applications reward students who are open, articulate and thoughtful about their journey. This may feel like a cultural shift – UK students are often more reserved in their writing – but it's important to highlight your strengths and share meaningful experiences.

Self-awareness, not self-promotion, is the key.

6. Show more than just academics

Universities want well-rounded applicants. Use your activities section to show how you've engaged with your interests outside the classroom – whether that's sport, music, part-time work, coding, mentoring or creative projects. Depth matters more than breadth.

7. Consider fit, not just rankings

Don't just aim for the 'top' names. Think about where you'll thrive – academically, socially and personally. Smaller liberal arts colleges, for example, may offer a better experience than a large Ivy League university, depending on your learning style and goals.

8. Watch out for language differences

Remember:

- 'Course' in the UK – 'module' in North America.
- 'Public school' in the US – state school (not Eton!).
- Spelling differences (organise v. organize) are fine – just be consistent with the style of the country you're applying to.

And always clarify terms like A levels, GCSEs or sixth form if used.

9. Budget carefully

Look into tuition, accommodation, travel and health insurance. Investigate scholarships and aid early, and don't assume North American study is unaffordable – some universities offer generous financial packages, especially those with large endowments.

10. Ask for support

This process can feel complex – but you're not expected to do it alone. Use your school's careers service, connect with alumni, reach out to admissions teams, and explore organisations like the Fulbright Commission (for US) and EduCanada. Many offer webinars, resources and one-to-one advice for UK students.

Adviser checklist

When guiding a student who is considering study in the US or Canada, encourage them to work through the steps below.

Understanding the appeal

- ☑ Consider the academic, cultural and personal benefits of studying in the US or Canada.
- ☑ Think about whether the liberal arts model, co-op programmes or research-intensive environments suit their goals.

Application systems

- ☑ Identify the correct application platform for each university (e.g. Common App, UC, OUAC).
- ☑ Check whether any universities require a direct application.

Plan ahead

- ☑ Review application deadlines for all relevant admission routes (Early Action, Early Decision, Regular Decision, Rolling Admissions).
- ☑ Create a timeline to manage essays, references, tests and financial aid forms.

Key application components
- [x] Understand what a holistic admissions process involves.
- [x] Gather academic transcripts covering GCSEs, A level predictions and Year 10–13 grades.
- [x] Check whether SAT, ACT or TOEFL scores are required, and register if necessary.

Essays and references
- [x] Develop a personal essay that reflects character, growth and personal insight.
- [x] Arrange for references from teachers or counsellors who know them well and can provide specific examples.

Academic presentation
- [x] Clarify how their UK qualifications map onto the North American grading system.
- [x] Ensure predicted grades and relevant qualifications are clearly explained.

Terminology and style
- [x] Familiarise themselves with key North American terms like GPA, major/minor and liberal arts.
- [x] Write in an appropriate tone – personal, reflective and authentic.

Understand student finances
- [x] Research tuition, accommodation and living costs for each institution.
- [x] Explore need-based and merit-based financial aid and scholarships.
- [x] Start preparing any required financial aid documents early.

Find the right fit
- [x] Reflect on the type of learning and social environment that will suit them.
- [x] Use student blogs, university websites and online tools to get a feel for different institutions.

Make the most of resources
- [x] Use platforms like Fulbright, EduCanada and BigFuture to guide their research.
- [x] Participate in university webinars, student panels or Q&A sessions.

Final checks
- [x] Consider how to present their academic and personal strengths in a way North American admissions officers will value.
- [x] Make sure that their choices reflect not only their academic ambitions but also their personal needs and goals.

FURTHER INFORMATION

For UK students considering study in the US or Canada, having the right information at your fingertips can make the process significantly easier. The resources below provide reliable guidance on application systems, planning tools, essay support, admissions testing and funding opportunities. While many tools are designed for all international applicants, the ones listed here are especially useful for students from the UK.

Application platforms

Most US universities accept applications through the Common App, available at www.commonapp.org, which allows students to apply to multiple institutions through a single system. It includes space for the main personal essay, activity list and teacher recommendations. In Canada, application platforms vary by province. Students applying to universities in Ontario will use the Ontario Universities' Application Centre (OUAC) at www.ouac.on.ca, while those applying in Alberta and British Columbia should visit www.applyalberta.ca and www.educationplannerbc.ca, respectively. In other provinces, applications are usually made directly to the institution.

Planning and research tools

The Fulbright Commission UK offers one of the most comprehensive guides for UK students applying to US universities. Available at www.fulbright.org.uk, the guide includes timelines, sample essays, financial aid advice and test preparation. Students considering Canadian universities should explore www.educanada.ca, the official government site, which outlines each province's systems and provides links to scholarship opportunities.

Another invaluable resource is BigFuture, run by the College Board, at www.bigfuture.collegeboard.org. It enables students to filter universities based on size, cost, subjects offered and admissions criteria – including whether standardised tests are optional.

Essay and testing support

Writing a North American university essay can feel unfamiliar, but resources like www.collegeessayguy.com offer detailed support, with free guides on brainstorming, structuring and editing essays that reflect personal voice and character.

If submitting standardised test scores, students can register and prepare through the official test sites. The SAT, run by the College Board, is at www.collegeboard.org, and the ACT can be accessed at www.act.org. For free, interactive SAT preparation, the Khan Academy platform (www.khanacademy.org/test-prep/sat) is endorsed by the College Board and provides practice questions, study plans and detailed feedback.

Financial aid and scholarships

Many US institutions use the CSS Profile, found at cssprofile.collegeboard.org, to assess eligibility for need-based financial aid. This form can be more detailed than UK equivalents and should be prepared well in advance.

UK students from lower-income backgrounds should also explore the Sutton Trust US Programme (www.suttontrust.com), which offers comprehensive support including mentoring, application coaching and funded visits to US campuses.

In Canada, students can consult the Universities Canada scholarship database at www.univcan.ca, which lists both institutional awards and external scholarships available to international students.

9 Alternative pathways: Broadening horizons beyond the traditional route

> **This chapter will:**
> - Explore alternative pathways to university, including gap years, internships and study-abroad programmes.
> - Outline how UK degrees with a year abroad work and their academic and personal benefits.
> - Navigate structured and self-sourced gap year options, including costs, visas and safeguarding considerations.
> - Detail how advisers can support students in finding and applying for international placements.
> - Review funding sources and case studies that highlight the impact of global experiences on student development.

Introduction

For many students, the end of secondary school or sixth-form college signals the beginning of university life. Yet this is by no means the only route to success. Increasingly, young people are choosing alternative pathways – ones that offer fresh perspectives, global experiences and personal growth beyond the confines of the conventional classroom. From gap years and international internships to UK degrees that include time abroad, these opportunities can be just as formative, if not more so, than the traditional route.

Work-readiness

Several organisations, including the Institute of Student Employers (ISE), the Chartered Management Institute (CMI) and the Sutton Trust, have voiced growing concern in recent years about the work-readiness of graduates. Employers frequently report that while academic qualifications remain important, many graduates are entering the workforce lacking essential attributes such as effective communication, adaptability, critical thinking and digital literacy. These so-called 'soft skills' have become even more critical in the post-pandemic workplace, where remote collaboration, resilience in the face of uncertainty and independent problem-solving are now routine expectations.

In response, there is a growing recognition that a more rounded educational journey – one that includes experiences beyond the classroom – can play a vital role in preparing students for the demands of modern employment. Non-traditional elements such as taking a structured gap year, completing a meaningful internship or participating in volunteering or enterprise projects can help to bridge the gap between academic learning and practical application. These experiences often develop initiative, interpersonal skills and professional confidence, offering a valuable counterbalance to the disrupted learning and reduced social interaction that characterised the education of many in the post-Covid-19 generation. As such, they are increasingly seen not as optional extras, but as integral to becoming truly 'work ready'. This chapter will provide advisers with the knowledge they need to address these concerns.

Study-abroad options within degree programmes

Many UK universities offer undergraduate degrees that include a year or semester abroad, formally known as 'sandwich courses'. These programmes allow students to combine academic study with international experience, helping them broaden their horizons and build valuable skills. Once largely the preserve of language students, these opportunities are now widely available in subjects ranging from politics and engineering to business, law and environmental science.

A year abroad can deepen subject knowledge through exposure to alternative teaching methods and academic approaches. Students may find themselves in smaller seminars, collaborative research environments with international students or interdisciplinary modules that challenge them to think in new ways. Equally important are the personal benefits: time spent living and learning in a different country helps students develop independence, adaptability and language skills. Many return with greater confidence, cultural awareness and a stronger sense of purpose.

While not every UK university offers international exchange opportunities, a significant majority do. Many have formal partnerships with overseas institutions, spanning more than 40 countries, including Australia, Japan, the US, Canada, Germany and Singapore.

The structure of these programmes varies. Some involve a full academic year spent at a partner institution, typically during the second or third year. Others are shorter semester-long exchanges or embedded within specific modules. Teaching is often in English, though language immersion is encouraged or required for certain courses.

Examples include the University of Portsmouth, which offers degrees such as International Relations and Languages with a year abroad in Europe or Latin America. Durham University has over 60 international partners and offers exchange options in disciplines including psychology, law and natural sciences. At the University of Manchester, students have access to nearly 300 partner institutions across 30 countries, while those at the University of Sussex can study sociology or geography in North America, Asia or Europe.

The University of Edinburgh offers exchanges across 300 institutions in nearly 40 countries, providing opportunities for students in most subject areas. Other universities offering well-established study-abroad options include University College London, King's College London, Queen's University Belfast and University of the Arts London, each of which has its own network of international partnerships and subject-specific exchanges. These schemes span a wide range of disciplines, including Fine Art, Design, History, Languages, Engineering and International Politics.

The importance of research

When researching programmes, students should consider the location and language of instruction, how the year fits into their overall course, and what support – financial, academic and pastoral – is available. Many universities reduce tuition fees for the year abroad, and initiatives such as the UK's Turing Scheme offer grants to help cover travel and living costs.

The benefits

Ultimately, studying abroad is about more than just coursework. It is a chance to explore new cultures, build a global network of peers and develop the skills needed to thrive in an increasingly international world. Whether it's biology in Brisbane, literature in Toronto or engineering in Singapore, the experience can add depth to a degree – and help shape a student's personal and professional future. For students seeking a different kind of learning experience before starting higher education, a structured gap year can be equally transformative and can potentially earn some funds to put towards living expenses while attending their future undergraduate course.

Structured gap year programmes

While some students head straight into higher education, others choose to take time out before university to explore alternative experiences. A well-structured gap year can be a powerful way to build confidence, clarify goals and gain meaningful life experience. A number of established schemes, both UK-based and international, offer students the chance to volunteer, learn new skills or travel with purpose. Some focus on education and leadership, while others are centred around sustainability, business, personal development or scientific research.

One popular option is **WWOOF** – Worldwide Opportunities on Organic Farms – which connects volunteers with organic farmers around the world. In exchange for work, participants are provided with accommodation and meals, making it a low-cost way to travel while learning about sustainable agriculture. It also offers cultural immersion and language development in rural communities and provides a practical grounding in environmentally responsible living.

Gapforce presents conservation-focused placements across the globe, including marine projects in Thailand, wildlife research in Costa Rica and outdoor adventure leadership training in Australia. These programmes typically last from two to twelve weeks and include accommodation, meals and support from in-country staff. They are particularly well suited to students with an interest in ecology, biology or environmental science and offer direct experience of the global challenges involved in preserving biodiversity and natural habitats.

Operation Wallacea is another organisation offering structured research-based gap year experiences. It runs biological and conservation science expeditions in locations such as Madagascar, Indonesia and South America. Participants work alongside academics and researchers, contributing to real-world environmental monitoring and data collection. These programmes are especially valuable for students considering degrees or careers in conservation, zoology, environmental science or marine biology. While they are fee-paying, the cost covers accommodation, specialist training, research supervision and logistics.

For students drawn to global citizenship and academic challenge, **Semester at Sea** provides an immersive study-abroad experience based aboard a ship, visiting multiple countries while students complete university-level coursework. The programme places a strong emphasis on sustainability, cross-cultural understanding and responsible travel. Although relatively costly, it provides a structured and supported environment for academic exploration and global learning.

Case study: Naomi — Operation Wallacea, Indonesia

Naomi was a Year 13 student with a strong academic profile in biology and geography. She had a clear interest in environmental science but was unsure whether she wanted to pursue it at university. She was particularly keen to take a gap year that combined travel with something meaningful — ideally fieldwork or scientific research.

After discussing several options, she was drawn to Operation Wallacea, particularly the biodiversity expedition in Sulawesi, Indonesia. She spent six weeks split between jungle and marine environments, supporting data collection on bird and butterfly populations, and later learning basic scuba diving to assist with coral reef monitoring. She worked alongside postgraduates from several universities and gained valuable insight into the realities of conservation work, her data ultimately being incorporated into the published research.

One of Naomi's major challenges was raising the funds to take part. The programme cost just over £3,000, and she worked part-time, organised a sponsored run, and set up a crowdfunding page (such as GoFundMe) to reach her target. The experience of planning and funding the trip, as well as navigating vaccinations, kit lists and travel logistics, gave her a sense of ownership before she had even departed.

On her return, Naomi found that the placement helped shape her personal statement for her university application. She was able to speak confidently about fieldwork techniques, global conservation issues and her own personal growth. She is now studying Environmental Science and hopes to return to field research during her degree. For Naomi, Operation Wallacea confirmed both her academic direction and her career ambition.

9 Alternative pathways: broadening horizons beyond the traditional route

> **Decision point**
>
> Naomi needed to decide how to use her gap year meaningfully – whether to travel, gain work experience or combine both through a structured programme. Operation Wallacea offered a unique blend of science, adventure and academic relevance.
>
> **Adviser insight**
>
> Advisers can guide students towards meaningful gap year experiences by helping them explore structured programmes linked to academic or career interests. Support with planning, budgeting and funding strategies can empower students to take ownership of the experience while building independence and resilience.

Commercial *v.* volunteer schemes

When planning a gap year, students can choose between commercial and volunteer-based schemes. Commercial programmes focus on professional development through paid placements, internships or research roles, often in business, science or technical fields, helping students build skills and boost employability. Volunteer schemes emphasise community service, personal growth and social impact, typically involving work with charities or schools in underserved areas. These may require participants to self-fund or fundraise. Both paths offer valuable experiences, serving different aims and personalities.

Some schemes centre on workplace readiness. **The Year in Industry** arranges paid, year-long UK placements in engineering, science, IT and business, offering hands-on experience in commercial or research settings. It suits students aiming for STEM or business degrees and is often competitive.

For international experience, **IAESTE** offers paid technical placements in over 80 countries, while **Erasmus+** traineeships remain accessible via select UK universities (e.g. the University of Edinburgh). **AIESEC** runs internships in business, IT and development; **DAAD's RISE scheme** funds summer research in Germany for science and engineering students. **UNITECH International** combines study and industry placements for engineering students across Europe, coordinated by ETH Zurich with partners like TU Delft and Politecnico di Milano. Other options include the **European Space Agency** and platforms such as **Europlacement** and **Globalplacement**.

Project Trust offers 8 or 12 month volunteer placements in Africa, Asia and Latin America, focusing on teaching, youth work and community development. These immersive roles cost around £6,000, to be raised by the participant.

Camp America enables UK students to work at US summer camps as counsellors or activity leaders. While less formal, it fosters leadership and cultural exchange. Participants receive subsidised travel, accommodation, food and pocket money, plus post-camp travel time.

City Year offers full-time placements in US schools, where volunteers act as mentors and tutors. The scheme builds leadership and communication skills and includes training, a stipend and an education grant.

Restless Development runs youth-led placements in countries such as Uganda, Nepal and Zambia, focusing on civic participation, health education, livelihoods and environmental campaigns.

CIEE Gap Year Abroad and **EF Gap Year** offer structured, fee-paying, multi-country experiences combining language learning, volunteering and internships. Programmes can include conservation in Costa Rica, sustainable farming in Japan or internships across Europe. Full-year packages cover tuition, travel and accommodation.

Each of these gap year options offers different benefits – some are academic, others focus on environmental or social impact, and many combine elements of both. Business, scientific and leadership-focused options are also well represented. Whether planting trees in the tropics, contributing to wildlife research, interning at a major company or taking part in a global voyage, students return with greater self-awareness, stronger communication skills and a broader sense of the world around them. Costs range from subsidised volunteer roles to full-fee structured programmes, but fundraising support and scholarships are often available. A purposeful gap year can be as enriching as any degree – offering not only time to reflect, but the opportunity to act and gain valuable experience of the world of work.

Table 9.1 compares commercial and volunteer gap year schemes, highlighting the key benefits and potential drawbacks of each.

Table 9.2 outlines a range of gap year programmes, showing the costs involved, the unique opportunities they offer students, and any key visa or eligibility considerations to keep in mind.

TABLE 9.1 Overall comparison – commercial v. volunteer schemes

Scheme type	Advantages	Disadvantages
Commercial	Paid placements reduce financial burden. Builds workplace skills valued by employers. Offers insight into specific careers (e.g. STEM, business). Enhances CV and university applications. Often includes mentoring or structured development.	Entry can be competitive. Focus may be narrow or sector-specific. Less emphasis on cultural immersion or community engagement.
Volunteer	Strong focus on personal growth and social impact. Opportunities to develop independence and empathy. Cultural immersion and global awareness. Builds soft skills (teamwork, communication, adaptability). Often flexible in design and location.	Often unpaid and can be expensive. May require substantial fundraising. Roles may lack formal structure or career alignment.

9 Alternative pathways: broadening horizons beyond the traditional route

TABLE 9.2 Summary of gap year programmes

Programme	Estimated cost	Advantage to student	Visa/eligibility notes
WWOOF	Low (£100–£500 for flights, plus insurance)	Hands-on sustainable farming, cultural immersion, language exposure.	Visa-free for short stays in many countries; may require tourist visa.
Gapforce	From ~£1,500 (2–12 weeks)	Conservation, adventure training, ecological awareness, team-based projects.	Tourist or volunteer visa depending on destination.
Operation Wallacea	£2,500–£4,000+ (varies by project)	Fieldwork experience in biology/conservation, academic contribution.	Short-term student/research or tourist visa usually required.
Semester at Sea	£20,000+ for full voyage	Study-abroad + global travel, academic credit, intercultural skills.	US visa + transit visas for ports of call.
The Year in Industry	Paid placement (students earn ~£12k)	Real-world experience in STEM/business, career insight, professional skills.	UK students; open to pre-university students aged 17+.
Project Trust	~£6,000 (fundraised)	Cultural immersion, long-term volunteering, personal growth.	Visa support provided by Project Trust based on placement country.
Camp America	Low upfront; travel subsidised; participant earns stipend	Work with children, independence, leadership, cultural exchange.	J-1 visa (provided via Camp America's sponsorship process).
City Year (US)	Low; living stipend provided	School-based mentoring, leadership training, education experience.	Typically requires US citizenship or residency; some exceptions.
Restless Development	Varies; often subsidised or grant-supported	Youth-led development, civic and community engagement, global awareness.	Visa requirements vary; organisation assists with arrangements.
CIEE Gap Year Abroad	From ~£8,000 (semester)	Language immersion, cultural exchange, structured homestays.	Student or cultural exchange visa required depending on country.
EF Gap Year	~£20,000+ (full year)	Multi-country experience, internships, service, language learning.	Visas for multiple destinations; EF provides visa guidance.

Case study: Mark — Camp America, US

Mark was preparing to begin his degree in Economics and Business when he approached the school's careers lead for advice about doing something productive during the summer before university. He was interested in working with children and had some volunteering experience at a local youth club. Camp America stood out as a good fit – offering cultural exchange, childcare experience and a structured environment abroad. He was also considering going into teaching and thought it would strengthen his application for a teaching qualification (PGCE or TEFL).

He applied independently, preparing a letter of application, recording a video introduction and gathering references from his teachers and the manager of the leisure centre where he worked as a lifeguard at the weekends. After being matched with a camp in upstate New York, he was offered a lifeguard role and also mentoring children aged 10 to 12. His responsibilities included cabin supervision, activity planning and shifts at the pool.

Mark described the experience as challenging but energising. Camp life was fast-paced and demanding, and he adapted quickly to working with a diverse staff team and managing young children in a residential setting. It was his first experience of dealing with neurodiverse children on the autistic spectrum, a skill which will undoubtedly come in useful later on. He developed confidence, flexibility and strong communication skills, and by the end of the summer was supporting newer staff and taking the lead in daily routines.

The programme provided food, accommodation and a modest stipend, and he was able to travel independently around the US for two weeks afterwards and visited California. While not a traditional gap year, the experience gave him a renewed sense of direction. Mark is now studying Economics and Business and has said that the confidence he built at camp has had a lasting impact on how he approaches group work, presentations and his future ambitions in teaching.

Decision point

Mark was unsure how best to spend the summer before university – whether to work locally, travel or pursue something more structured. Camp America offered a balance of paid experience, cultural exchange and personal development.

Adviser insight

Shorter international placements can be ideal for students not taking a full gap year but seeking experience before university. Advisers can help students assess suitability, prepare applications and reflect on how skills gained link to future study or career plans.

9 Alternative pathways: broadening horizons beyond the traditional route

Advising students on self-sourced international work placements

While many students benefit from structured gap year or study-abroad programmes, there is growing interest in self-sourced international work placements. These placements – when researched and arranged independently – can also be highly valuable, offering unique opportunities for growth, maturity and real-world experience. With the right preparation and support, students can turn a self-arranged placement into a rich and rewarding pathway. Teachers or advisers have a key role to play in guiding this process, helping students develop a clear plan, remain realistic and ensure that appropriate safeguards are in place.

Students who find and secure their own placement abroad gain far more than work experience. They develop resilience, initiative and independence, all of which are essential for success in both university and employment. From the very start, they are required to manage communications across time zones and cultures, advocate for themselves and adapt to unfamiliar professional settings. These skills – combined with the insight that comes from immersion in another culture – can build confidence, cultural fluency and a stronger sense of direction. Even unsuccessful applications offer valuable learning and reflection.

Case study: Simon — automotive internship in Germany

Simon had long shown an interest in Mechanical Engineering but was uncertain whether to go straight to university or gain practical experience first. Through his school's careers adviser, he learnt about the possibility of arranging a self-sourced international placement. His mother, who works in marketing for Volkswagen from home in the UK, introduced him to a contact at the company's Stuttgart headquarters, which led to an application for a year-long internship in the automotive sector.

Over the course of 12 months, Simon was based in the company's powertrain development division, supporting quality assurance and testing processes. He shadowed engineers, contributed to team meetings and took part in a research project focused on improving energy efficiency in hybrid engines. His team praised his enthusiasm, adaptability and attention to detail. He quickly settled into the rhythm of the working environment and adapted to using German as the language of day-to-day communication.

The internship was unpaid, but the company provided subsidised accommodation and meals, and Simon funded the remainder through part-time work and a small grant from a local travel bursary scheme. Living independently in Germany helped him develop confidence, budgeting skills and cultural awareness, while his placement offered a clearer view of what a career in engineering might involve.

Simon is now studying Mechanical Engineering at university and remains in contact with his former supervisors. His experience in Germany not only gave him strong material for his personal statement and interviews, but also confirmed his interest in automotive design and international collaboration. He is now planning to apply for a summer internship with a European engineering firm in his second year.

Decision point

Simon had to choose between going directly to university or taking a year out to gain hands-on industry experience abroad – a choice that involved weighing up academic timelines, financial implications and long-term career goals.

Adviser insight

When students are considering self-sourced placements, advisers can help them identify personal networks, support professional communication (e.g. CVs, letters) and manage practical arrangements like funding and language preparation. These experiences often clarify academic direction and strengthen applications.

International apprenticeships for UK-based students

While most apprenticeships are tied to national education systems and limited to residents, a small number of structured, internationally oriented programmes are open to UK-based school leavers. These offer a rare opportunity to combine on-the-job training with global experience, often leading to recognised qualifications and paid employment.

Airbus UK apprenticeships with international exposure

Airbus runs a well-established apprenticeship scheme in the UK, with training delivered at sites such as Filton and Broughton. Opportunities exist in engineering, manufacturing, IT, supply chain and business functions. Apprentices are employed full-time (starting salary around £16,000 per year, rising annually) and study part-time for qualifications such as a Higher National Certificate (HNC), Foundation Degree or full bachelor's degree, depending on the role and level.

While the scheme is primarily UK-based, some advanced and degree-level apprentices may be considered for short-term placements at Airbus facilities in other European countries – for example, in France or Germany on a case-by-case basis through internal mobility programmes. These placements are not guaranteed and depend on role requirements and business needs.

UNITECH International

Aimed at engineering undergraduates, UNITECH combines academic study with industrial placements across multiple European countries. UK-based applicants can apply through participating institutions such as the University of Warwick or the University of Southampton. The programme includes a semester abroad and a paid international internship at a partner company (e.g. ABB, Hilti or Siemens). While not an apprenticeship in the formal UK sense, it provides structured work experience, professional training and leadership development alongside degree study. Internship salaries vary by country and company.

Supporting students to find a placement

One of the most important forms of support advisers can offer is helping students to prepare a strong CV and a professional, tailored letter of application. These documents should be clearly written, well structured and adapted for an international audience. Language should be plain and direct, with a focus on transferable skills such as teamwork, initiative, communication and language ability. Application letters should demonstrate genuine interest in the organisation, outline what the student hopes to gain, and explain what they can contribute.

How can advisers help?

Advisers may wish to provide templates on platforms such as Canva or direct students to tools like Unifrog's CV builder, which offers structured guidance to help them present themselves confidently and effectively. Running short CV-writing clinics in school can also be a valuable way to build students' confidence.

A popular activity for older students, if you have lesson time with them, is a mock internship challenge, inspired by *The Apprentice* TV show. Students create a CV and covering letter and submit these to a teacher acting as the recruiter for a fictitious placement with a well-known employer such as WWF or Deloitte. Candidates then take part in a mock interview, and a winner is selected based on their overall performance. Where possible, schools might invite a local employer to help judge the entries and interviews.

This activity allows students to practise essential skills – from writing applications to handling interviews – in a supportive environment. These skills can then be applied when seeking actual placements or part-time roles.

When helping students identify suitable real-life placements, advisers can suggest they begin with a broad area of interest – such as environmental science, marketing, education or tourism – and research organisations working in those fields, including international options. It is important for students to have a realistic understanding of the opportunities available, taking into account their age, language ability and experience. One-to-one meetings with advisers can help manage expectations and shape their search.

Often, placements with local charities, community groups, schools or small businesses are more accessible and offer more hands-on experience than those with larger global firms. The skills developed through local experience – including CV writing, communication and professionalism – are highly transferable and can support future applications for international placements.

Experiencing more internationally

Reaching out to personal contacts is also an important strategy. Students should be encouraged to talk to friends, family and local community networks who may have international connections. Many placements come about through informal channels – such as a parent's contact who runs a hotel in Spain, or a family friend working at an NGO abroad. This can provide some beneficial insights, as some countries will allow interns more in-depth experience, as their health and safety regulations are a little more flexible than those in the UK. For example, high school interns for Medicine in Thailand are allowed to view surgery, while properly supervised, not something which could be contemplated in the UK. While not every contact will lead to a confirmed placement, these conversations can open up possibilities that students might not find online.

Due diligence

Advisers should also remind students and their parents of the importance of due diligence. Not all informal or international opportunities will have clear structures in place. Where students are seeking their own placements, especially those involving working with children, vulnerable adults or within schools or healthcare settings, issues around safeguarding, supervision and public liability insurance must be considered carefully. Students and families should be encouraged to check what cover is provided by the host organisation, and consider whether additional insurance is needed. Where students are under 18, it is especially important to clarify who will be responsible for their welfare and to ensure a named adult is available on site.

Visa requirements

Visa requirements are another important area for consideration. UK-based students will need to check whether they are eligible to undertake paid or unpaid work, internships or voluntary roles in the host country. Most countries distinguish between volunteering and employment, and students cannot legally be paid for their work unless they hold a passport from that country or have secured a suitable work visa. In some cases, students may be permitted to receive accommodation, meals or limited expenses without breaching visa conditions. It is essential that students and families check the latest guidance for the country in question and understand what is permitted under the relevant visa category. Embassies, consulates and official immigration websites are the most reliable sources of current advice.

Staying organised

Because applying for placements is a process that often involves multiple emails, follow-ups and timelines, advisers or teachers can help students stay organised by suggesting they keep a spreadsheet or application tracker. This should record the name of the organisation, whom they contacted, the date of the application, status of response and any agreed follow-up. This not only helps students stay on top of their progress but also allows advisers to monitor the process and offer guidance when needed. Students may electronically share the spreadsheet with staff for monitoring purposes, or the teacher can check drafts of letters or CVs before they are sent. This will be a dry run for students when it comes to their graduate employment applications.

Supporting students to arrange their own work placements overseas can be one of the most meaningful areas of adviser involvement. Even if a placement does not ultimately materialise, the act of researching, writing, reaching out and responding to feedback builds practical skills and self-awareness. With encouragement, structure and a shared understanding of safety, planning and legal requirements, advisers can help students approach the world with confidence – and shape a purposeful and independent path forward.

Understanding the Turing Scheme

Following the UK's departure from the Erasmus+ programme in 2020 due to Brexit, the UK Government introduced a new global mobility scheme known as the Turing Scheme. Launched in 2021, it provides funding to support UK students to study, work or train abroad as part of their education. Unlike Erasmus+, which was a reciprocal programme rooted in EU partnership, the Turing Scheme focuses solely on outbound mobility and is open to students from across higher education, further education and vocational pathways.

The scheme is designed to widen access to international opportunities. A particular emphasis is placed on students from disadvantaged or underrepresented backgrounds, with additional funding available to help cover travel, insurance and living costs. While Erasmus+ placements were mostly limited to European countries, the Turing Scheme supports exchanges and placements in more than 160 countries worldwide – including the US, Japan, Canada, Australia and South Africa.

UK universities, colleges and schools apply for funding on behalf of their students. Successful applicants can take part in academic exchanges, internships or research placements lasting from a few weeks to a full academic year. Although the revised scheme has allowed for a broader international focus, it has also meant that some long-standing EU partnerships have needed to be renegotiated independently, and students may now face more complex visa or administrative processes, particularly within Europe.

Despite these changes, the Turing Scheme offers students an ambitious, globally focused alternative to Erasmus+, with opportunities to gain valuable international experience in a wide range of academic, professional and cultural settings.

What does the data say?

In higher education, study abroad remains a smaller but significant route. In the 2019–20 academic year, 36,225 UK students engaged in study or work placements abroad as part of their degree programme – representing around 1.5% of the total student population (Universities UK International, 2021). Following the UK's departure from the Erasmus+ scheme, the government introduced the Turing Scheme in 2021 to support outward global mobility. In the 2023/24 academic year, nearly 23,000 higher education students from the UK received Turing Scheme funding to undertake placements overseas (Universities UK International, 2024).

Participation in gap years

Recent data shows that gap years continue to be a popular option among UK students. In 2023, it was estimated that between 183,000 and 232,000 students aged 18 to 24 took a gap year, with approximately 30,970 deferring their university entry in the 2022/23 academic year – a 28% increase from 2012, though slightly down from the post-pandemic peak in 2021. Among gap year participants, an estimated 83% undertook work within the UK, while 16% worked or volunteered abroad (Teaching Abroad Direct, using UCAS and HESA data).

Sources of funding

Some students successfully apply for bursaries, sponsorships or local grants to pay for their experience, while others fundraise through part-time work or community events. It is worth exploring whether a scheme offers financial support or guidance on raising funds, as this can significantly broaden access to programmes that might otherwise seem out of reach to some families. Organisations such as the Jack Petchey Foundation, the Rotary Club, and the Lord Mayor's 800th Anniversary Awards Trust have been known to support young people with funding for international experiences. Some local councils and sixth-form colleges also offer travel bursaries or discretionary funds, and students should be encouraged to explore regional sources of support alongside national schemes. The schemes listed are open to UK students, though some have regional restrictions or require applications through a school or local organisation. The Turing Scheme is open nationally but must be applied for by the student's school or college. Many prioritise applicants from lower-income backgrounds.

Looking ahead

Choosing an alternative pathway after school – whether through studying abroad or taking a structured gap year – can be one of the most rewarding decisions a student makes. These experiences offer more than a change of scenery; they provide space to grow, challenge assumptions and build a deeper understanding of the world.

9 Alternative pathways: broadening horizons beyond the traditional route

Whether through a conservation project in Costa Rica, a semester in Japan or a year mentoring in a US classroom, students gain valuable skills and insight that can shape their future direction. For teachers and advisers supporting families, the key is to keep an open mind and support students in choosing a path that reflects their interests, ambitions and values. With careful planning and a sense of curiosity, stepping off the traditional route can lead to personal growth, academic strength and a clearer sense of purpose.

Adviser checklist

Highlight the value of alternative routes
- [x] Emphasise that gap years, study abroad and internships can offer equal or greater benefits compared to the traditional university path.

Encourage research into year abroad options
- [x] Help students explore degrees that include a year abroad and understand their structure, costs and academic integration.

Promote structured gap year planning
- [x] Guide students to reputable programmes that align with their interests and career goals, and advise on logistics like visas, safeguarding and insurance.

Advise on funding strategies
- [x] Support students in identifying bursaries, fundraising opportunities and low-cost placement options.

Discuss personal development benefits
- [x] Reinforce how experiences like volunteering, internships and cultural immersion develop transferable skills and independence.

Support CV and application preparation
- [x] Assist students with writing international-standard CVs and covering letters tailored to self-sourced placements.

Champion equity of access
- [x] Encourage students from all backgrounds to explore global experiences and highlight inclusive schemes like the Turing Scheme.

Promote responsible planning
- [x] Ensure students consider safety, supervision, legal responsibilities and realistic expectations when planning placements abroad.

FURTHER INFORMATION

WWOOF – www.wwoof.net

Gapforce – www.gapforce.org

Operation Wallacea – www.opwall.com

Semester at Sea – www.semesteratsea.org

The Year in Industry – www.etrust.org.uk/the-year-in-industry

Project Trust – www.projecttrust.org.uk

Camp America – www.campamerica.co.uk

City Year – www.cityyear.org

Restless Development – www.restlessdevelopment.org

CIEE Gap Year Abroad – www.ciee.org

EF Gap Year – www.efgapyear.com

Turing Scheme – https://www.gov.uk/government/publications/turing-scheme-international-study-and-work-placements/overview-of-the-turing-scheme

Prospects – www.prospects.ac.uk

Year Out Group – www.yearoutgroup.org

Go Overseas – www.gooverseas.com

Teaching Abroad Direct – www.teachingabroaddirect.co.uk

The Gap Network – www.thegapnetwork.org

Letz Live – www.letzlive.org

10 Navigating costs and financial aid

This chapter will:

- Explain the full cost of attending university abroad, including tuition, living expenses, hidden extras and visa-related costs.
- Compare tuition and living costs across major study destinations, using a structured table and country-specific examples.
- Outline the main types of financial aid available, including merit-based, need-based and government or institutional scholarships.
- Clarify the rules on student work rights by country, including weekly hour limits, permit requirements and typical job types.
- Detail visa requirements, proof of funds and residency-related fee categories to help families plan realistically and avoid unexpected costs.

Introduction: Affordability

For many families, the most pressing question in the university application process is not where to go, but how to afford it. As tuition fees rise and the cost of living continues to climb globally, financing higher education has become a complex challenge. Yet with the right knowledge, forward planning and awareness of the support available, studying abroad can be more affordable than it first appears. This chapter breaks down the true cost of university, demystifies different types of financial aid and provides country-specific insights to help families make informed decisions.

The real cost of university abroad

When planning to study internationally, many families focus first on tuition fees – but this is just one piece of a much larger picture. To make truly informed decisions, you'll need to understand the total cost of attendance, which includes not just tuition but also living expenses, administrative fees, travel, insurance and day-to-day spending. These costs vary significantly by country, city and university, but a structured overview can help you compare options with clarity.

What 'cost of attendance' really means

The full cost of university is typically broken down into:

- Tuition fees – the amount paid to attend courses and access academic facilities.
- Living costs – accommodation, food, local travel, utilities, internet, clothing.
- Hidden extras – including:
  1. Visa and residence permit fees.
  2. Travel to and from your home country.
  3. Health insurance (mandatory in many countries).
  4. Books, stationery and academic materials.
  5. Personal expenses and social activities.

In countries where tuition is relatively low or even free, living costs and visa requirements can still make a major financial impact. The key is to consider total affordability, not just headline tuition figures.

Table 10.1 offers a summary of estimated annual tuition and living costs for international students in selected countries. All £ approximations are based on exchange rates at the time of writing and are for guidance only. Actual costs will vary depending on university, subject, city and currency fluctuations.

Subject-based variation

It's also important to note that tuition varies by subject:

- Medicine, Dentistry, Engineering and Architecture are typically more expensive.
- Humanities, Languages and Social Sciences are usually at the lower end of the fee scale.
- At the University of Sydney, for example, international students pay over AUD 85,000 per year for Medicine, while Arts degrees are closer to AUD 40,000.

This comprehensive view of real university costs sets the stage for understanding how families can fund these expenses – through scholarships, grants and well-informed planning – which we'll explore in the next section.

Types of financial aid

Paying for university is rarely a one-source solution. Most students and families rely on a mix of scholarships, grants and work opportunities. Knowing the differences – and how to access them – is key.

Merit-based aid

Merit-based scholarships are awarded to students who demonstrate excellence – academic, athletic, artistic or leadership-based. They are not dependent on family income.

- Automatic v. application-required: Some universities automatically consider applicants; others require a separate form, personal statement or portfolio.

10 Navigating costs and financial aid

TABLE 10.1 Comparative overview: Tuition and living costs by country

Country	Tuition (local currency)	Tuition (£ approx.)	Living costs (£ approx.)	Notes
United States	$30,000–$80,000	£24,000–£64,000	£8,000–£12,000	Highest fees; aid widely available.
United Kingdom	£11,000–£38,000 (note this is the fee range for international students in the UK; the maximum fee for home students is £9,535/year)	—	£10,000–£12,800	Wide range; medicine most expensive.
Germany	Mostly free; €100–€350 semester fee	£0–£2,600	£8,800–£10,400	Free tuition at most public universities.
Netherlands	€6,000–€15,000 (non-EU); €2,530 (EU)	£5,200–£13,000	£9,600–£11,200	Many English-taught programmes; good scholarship options.
Spain	€800–€3,500 (public); €5,000–€20,000 (private)	£700–£17,400	£6,400–£8,800	Very affordable for EU students.
Australia	AUD 20,000–45,000	£10,400–£23,400	£11,200–£13,600	High cost of living; good scholarships.
Canada	CAD 15,000–30,000	£8,800–£17,600	£6,400–£8,800	Strong value and post-study options.
Singapore	SGD 20,000–40,000	£9,600–£19,200	£6,000–£12,000	Tuition Grant available; must work in Singapore after.
Hong Kong	HKD 140,000–265,000	£14,400–£27,600	£5,100–£10,200	Strong scholarships; high cost of housing.
Japan/South Korea/ Malaysia/Taiwan	$3,000–$10,000 (varies)	£2,400–£8,000	£4,800–£9,600	Lower tuition; many government scholarships.
Nordic Countries (EU students)	Mostly free	£0	£10,400–£12,800	Free tuition; high living costs.
Nordic Countries (non-EU)	€8,000–€15,000	£7,000–£13,000	£10,400–£12,800	Tuition for non-EU students; limited scholarships.

Note:
For UK students (and eligible EU or Irish students under residency agreements), tuition fees at public universities in England are capped at £9,535 per year. This fee level changed for the 2025–26 academic year, and is expected to increase annually with inflation in the future. Separate fee structures apply in Scotland, Wales and Northern Ireland.

- Examples: President's Scholarship (Canada), NUS Merit Scholarship (Singapore), various US university 'Dean's List' awards.
- Sustainability: Many merit awards are renewable each year if the student maintains strong academic performance.

Need-based aid

Need-based aid is awarded based on a family's financial situation. These are more common in the US and Canada, but some other international universities also offer them.

- Expected Family Contribution (EFC): In the US/Canada, this is the amount a family is expected to contribute, calculated using detailed financial forms (like the CSS Profile).
- Documentation: Often includes tax returns, income statements, bank records and information about family assets.
- Need-blind v. need-aware:
    1. *Need-blind*: Admission is decided without considering ability to pay; aid is offered to meet the gap.
    2. *Need-aware*: Financial need may influence admission decisions, especially when budgets are tight.

Government and institutional scholarships

Many governments and individual universities offer structured scholarship schemes:

- DAAD (Germany): Broad range of academic scholarships for international students.
- Australia Awards: Covers full tuition and living costs for students from selected countries.
- MEXT (Japan): Government scholarships covering fees, travel and stipend.
- Turing Scheme/Erasmus+: Funding for UK/EU students studying abroad.
- HK SAR Government Scholarship: Up to HKD 80,000 per year for non-local students.
- Singapore Tuition Grant: Reduces tuition in exchange for post-study work obligation.

Regional and country-specific scholarships

Some scholarships are offered based on geography or diplomatic partnerships:

- Belt and Road Scholarships: Available to students from specific Asian countries.
- APEC Scholarships: Support for students from Pacific Rim nations.
- Commonwealth Scholarships: For students from Commonwealth countries to study in other member nations.

In the next section, we explore what this looks like in practice: how much aid is typically offered, who qualifies and what it takes to apply successfully.

Country snapshots: What to expect

Every country offers a different combination of tuition fees, living expenses, scholarships, visa rules and work opportunities. Here's what students and families can expect in some of the most popular international study destinations, presented as a practical guide to comparative decision-making.

In the **United States,** tuition costs remain among the highest globally. Public universities can charge up to $40,000 (approx. £31,500) per year, while private colleges often exceed $75,000 (approx. £59,000). Add another $10,000–$15,000 (approx. £8,000–£12,000) for living expenses, and the full cost becomes significant. However, the US also offers a vast range of scholarships – both merit and need-based – with over 250 institutions providing full-ride awards. Some of the most prestigious universities operate on a need-blind basis, ensuring that students are admitted regardless of financial means. Visa applicants must prove they can fund their first year. Work rights are limited to on-campus employment during term time, with programmes like OPT (Optional Practical Training) available post-graduation.

Canada presents a more moderate picture. Tuition fees typically range from CAD 15,000–30,000 (approx. £9,000–£18,000), with living costs around CAD 10,000–15,000 (approx. £6,000–£9,000). Students can apply for institutional scholarships, provincial aid and research stipends. A study visa requires evidence of tuition funding and at least CAD 10,000 for living expenses. Students can work up to 20 hours per week during term and full-time during scheduled breaks. A generous post-study work visa is available for up to three years.

Germany stands out for offering free tuition at most public universities. Some regions, such as Baden-Württemberg, charge around €1,500 (approx. £1,300) per semester to non-EU students. Living expenses average around €10,200–12,000 (approx. £8,700–£10,200) per year. The DAAD and various regional scholarships, including the Baden-Württemberg Stipendium, are available. Visa applicants must show they have access to around €10,332, usually held in a blocked account. Non-EU students are allowed to work 120 full or 240 half-days per year.

In the **Netherlands,** tuition for non-EU students ranges from €6,000 to €15,000 (approx. £5,100–£12,700), while EU students benefit from the lower statutory rate of €2,530 (approx. £2,100). Living costs hover between €11,000 and €13,000 (approx. £9,400–£11,100). Popular scholarships include the Holland Scholarship and the Orange Tulip Scholarship. Students must demonstrate they can cover tuition and living expenses when applying for a visa. Work is allowed up to 16 hours per week during term, and full-time during holidays – though a work permit is required.

Spain is often considered one of the more affordable options. Public university tuition ranges from €800 to €3,500 (approx. £700–£3,000), with private institutions costing up to €20,000 (approx. £17,000). Living costs are relatively low, particularly in cities outside Madrid and Barcelona. Eligible students benefit from EU funding programmes like Erasmus+, as well as university-level aid. Visa applicants need to show proof of funding and valid health insurance. Work is permitted up to 20 hours per week during term with a permit.

In **Australia**, tuition ranges between AUD 20,000 and 45,000 (approx. £10,500–£24,000), and living costs average AUD 21,000–25,000 (approx. £11,000–£13,000). Scholarships like the Australia Awards and various university grants provide financial relief. To secure a student visa, students must demonstrate sufficient financial capacity. They can work up to 48 hours per fortnight during term and full-time during holidays.

New Zealand has similar structures. Tuition generally falls between NZD 22,000–32,000 (approx. £10,500–£15,000), with living costs estimated at NZD 20,000–25,000 (approx. £9,500–£12,000). Government and institutional scholarships are widely available. Students must show proof of NZD 20,000 in support funds when applying for a visa. They may work up to 20 hours per week during term and full-time in holiday periods.

In **Singapore**, tuition costs range from SGD 20,000 to 40,000 (approx. £12,000–£24,000), and living expenses from SGD 10,000 to 20,000 (approx. £6,000–£12,000). Scholarships like the NUS Merit Scholarship and the government's Tuition Grant Scheme (which carries a post-graduation work obligation) are common. A valid Student Pass allows up to 16 hours of work per week during term.

Hong Kong combines high tuition – typically between HKD 140,000 and 265,000 (approx. £14,000–£26,000) – with substantial scholarship support. Awards include the HK SAR Government Scholarship and funding through the Belt and Road and APEC programmes. Living expenses range from HKD 50,000 to 100,000 (approx. £5,000–£10,000) annually. Work is permitted in on-campus or internship-related roles.

The East Asian region – including **Japan, South Korea, Malaysia and Taiwan** – generally offers lower tuition fees, often between $3,000 and $10,000 (approx. £2,400–£8,000) per year. Living costs are modest compared to Western Europe or North America. Generous government scholarships are available: Japan's MEXT, Korea's GKS and Malaysia's Ministry of Higher Education awards among them. Work rights typically allow students to work part-time under specific conditions, often with employer approval or reporting.

Finally, in the **Nordic countries** of Finland, Sweden and Denmark, tuition is free for EU/EEA students. For non-EU students, tuition can range from €8,000 to €15,000 (approx. £6,800–£12,700). Living costs are high – €12,000 to €15,000 (approx. £10,200–£12,700) annually – and students must show they can support themselves when applying for a visa. Scholarships are offered at both university and national levels. Work rights vary slightly: students in Finland may work up to 25 hours per week, while in Sweden and Denmark the limit is 20 hours.

Figure 10.1 illustrates the relationship between average international tuition fees and typical financial aid across major study destinations. Countries like the US and Singapore combine high tuition with generous scholarships, while Germany and Spain offer low-cost education with minimal aid. The UK and Nordic countries charge high fees but offer limited financial support, making them comparatively expensive for self-funded students. Mid-range options like Canada, Australia and the Netherlands balance moderate costs with accessible funding. Overall, the graph highlights the importance of looking beyond headline fees to consider the value and availability of financial aid when planning to study abroad.

10 Navigating costs and financial aid

FIGURE 10.1 Average tuition fee v. typical subsidy/aid by country (GBP).

Note: Figures are indicative averages only and may vary by institution, study level and residency status.
Source: Compiled using data from EducationData.org (Hanson, 2025); OECD, Education at a Glance 2024; UNESCO, Global Education Monitoring Report 2024.

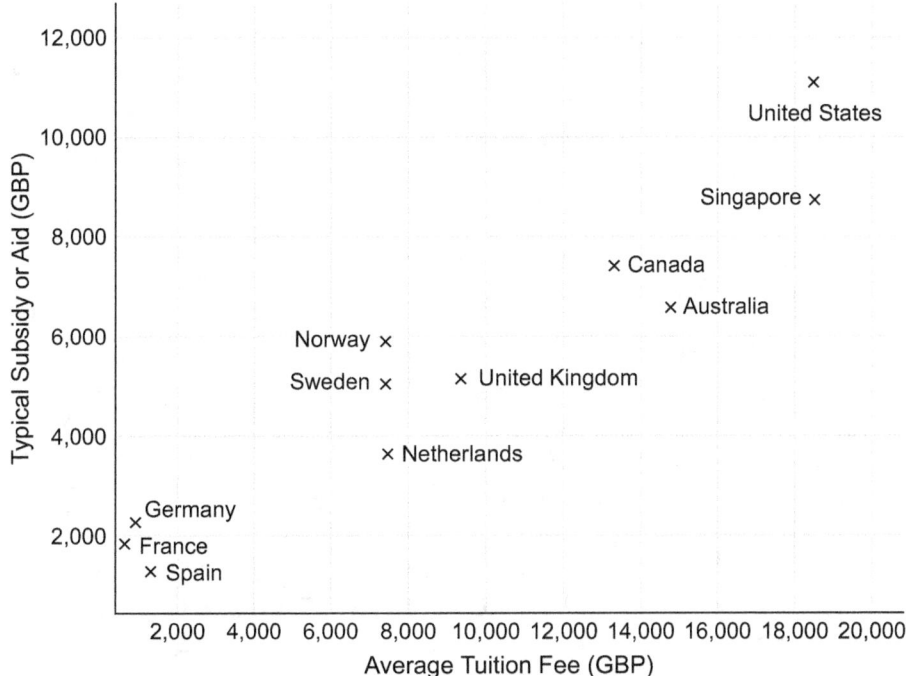

Figure 10.2 (overleaf) compares average annual undergraduate tuition fees for international students in key study destinations, offering a snapshot of relative costs worldwide.

How to find and apply for scholarships

Finding and applying for scholarships can be time-consuming, but it's one of the most important parts of making study abroad affordable. Each year, millions of pounds in scholarship funding go unclaimed – often because students aren't aware of the opportunities available or miss crucial deadlines. According to SoFi, nearly $100 million in scholarships and over $2 billion in grants are left unclaimed annually due to a lack of applicants (SoFi, 2025). This section explains where to look, what to expect and how to prepare a successful application.

Start with university sources

Every university has a financial aid or international admissions page where scholarships are listed. Some are awarded automatically based on academic merit, while others require a separate application.

FIGURE 10.2 Typical annual undergraduate tuition fees for international students (GBP).

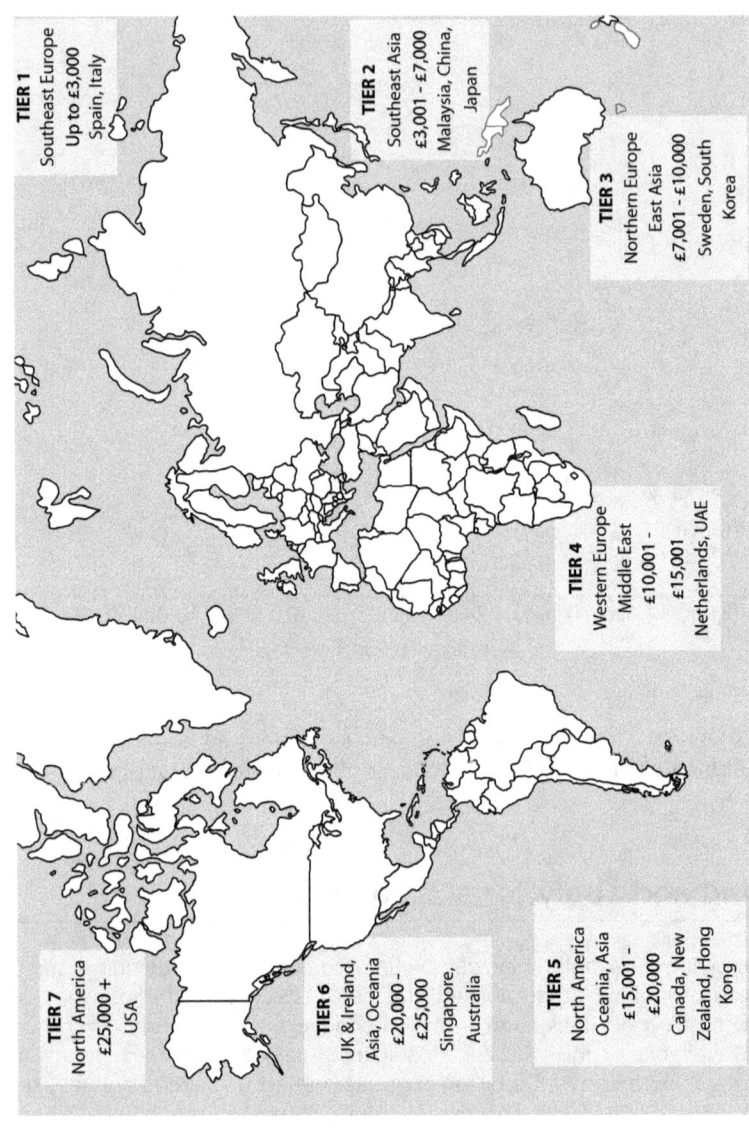

Note: Actual costs vary by country, institution, course and residency status. Figures exclude living expenses and are intended as a general guide.
Sources: British Council. 2024. *Study Abroad Tuition Fees Overview*; UNESCO. 2024. *Global Education Monitoring Report*; StudyPortals. 2024. *Average Tuition Fees by Country*. Cross-referenced with official national university portals (2024/25).
This map has been adapted from https://commons.wikimedia.org/wiki/File:Blank_Map_of_The_World_Small_Scale_Without_Borders_Mercator_Projection.png, which is licensed under the Creative Commons Attribution-ShareAlike 4.0 International license.

- Look for both institutional and departmental awards.
- Don't overlook small-value scholarships – these can add up and often have fewer applicants.
- Contact the admissions or international office if criteria are unclear.

Use global scholarship databases
- Unifrog's Special Opportunities tool: A tailored database that filters scholarships, summer schools and extracurricular awards by eligibility.
- ScholarshipPortal (EU) and DAAD.de (Germany): Comprehensive lists of European and German scholarships.
- ScholarshipsCanada.com, IEFA.org, and EducationUSA: Country-specific search tools.

Track requirements and deadlines
- Some scholarships are automatic with application; others have separate forms, essays or financial disclosures. Often the scholarship application runs in parallel with the place consideration, if they are not directly linked.
- Create a timeline for when to complete and submit each component (ideally by early Year 13).
- Ensure you know whether applications require references, transcripts, proof of income or other documents.

Tips for a strong application
- Personal Statement: Write clearly about your goals, values and how the scholarship supports your future.
- References: Choose referees who know you well and can speak to both academic and character strengths.
- Proofread: Typos and vague answers can undermine strong qualifications.

Watch for red flags
- Legitimate scholarships never charge a fee to apply.
- Be cautious of third-party 'agencies' offering guaranteed scholarships – always verify through official university or government channels.

Case study: Amrit — sports scholarship to the US

Amrit had always dreamed of studying in the US, inspired by the combination of academic prestige and high-performance sport. As a talented track and field athlete, he saw university as a place to grow both intellectually and athletically – but the costs initially seemed out of reach.

After researching funding options, Amrit discovered that many US universities offer sports scholarships covering full or partial tuition, accommodation and even meal plans. With guidance from his school's careers adviser, he began preparing a competitive application: registering with the NCAA Eligibility Center, compiling a sports CV and performance video and researching universities with strong track and field programmes.

He applied to a range of institutions with competitive athletics programmes, tailoring each application to the athletic and academic fit. Several months later, he received a full scholarship offer from Indiana Tech in the Midwest, covering tuition, housing and a living stipend.

The scholarship came with commitments – maintaining a minimum GPA, training year-round and travelling to competitions – but it opened the door to a life-changing experience.

'If I'd looked only at the cost, I might have given up,' Amrit reflects. 'But once I knew where to look and what to show, it all started to fall into place.'

Decision point

Amrit had to weigh several key decision points. He wanted to find a university that supported his sport without compromising academic goals and compared the opportunities available across different athletic associations and programme levels. Some universities offered partial funding, while others included housing, insurance or additional stipends. He also took into account location, climate and distance from home.

Adviser insight

His school careers adviser played a crucial role, helping Amrit understand the eligibility process, refine outreach emails to coaches and select appropriate institutions. Early preparation was essential. By starting in Year 11, Amrit was able to compile high-quality footage, track performance stats and meet application deadlines well ahead of time.

In the US, athletic scholarships are typically offered through university sports departments and funded through a combination of institutional resources and revenue from athletics. Programmes in high-profile sports tend to offer the most generous awards, but strong support can also be found at mid-sized universities, smaller institutions and across different athletic associations.

For Amrit, the scholarship not only made study in the US possible but also provided a launchpad for both academic and personal development on an international scale.

Working while studying

Part-time work is a valuable way for students to supplement their finances while studying abroad. It can help cover living costs, provide real-world experience and enhance employability after graduation. However, work rights for international students vary significantly by country, and students must be careful to comply with visa conditions.

Table 10.2 compares work hour limits for international students across different study destinations, highlighting the maximum term-time allowances and key conditions to be aware of.

TABLE 10.2 Work hour limits by country. Most countries place limits on the number of hours international students can work during term time.

Country	Work hour limit
United Kingdom	Up to 20 hours/week during term; full-time in holidays.
Australia	Up to 48 hours/fortnight during term; full-time in breaks.
Canada	Up to 20 hours/week during term; full-time in holidays (no limit from 2024).
United States	Up to 20 hours/week on-campus (F-1 visa); off-campus work via CPT/OPT.
Germany	Up to 120 full or 240 half-days/year.
Netherlands	Up to 16 hours/week; work permit required.
Spain	Up to 20 hours/week; employer must apply for permit.
Singapore	Up to 16 hours/week; only with a valid Student's Pass.
Finland	Up to 25 hours/week during term.
Sweden	Up to 20 hours/week.
Denmark	Up to 20 hours/week.
New Zealand	Up to 20 hours/week during term; full-time in holidays.
Japan	Up to 28 hours/week during term; work permit required.
South Korea	Up to 20 hours/week; employer reporting required.
Malaysia	Up to 20 hours/week; only during semester breaks.
Taiwan	Up to 20 hours/week; permit required.
Hong Kong	On-campus work only; internships allowed under conditions.
Norway	Up to 20 hours/week.

These limits are outlined in UKCISA guidance, which also advises caution around employer contracts and term-time work (UKCISA, n.d.).

Types of student jobs

Common student roles include:

- On-campus jobs (library assistant, barista, administrative support, exam invigilator);
- Retail or hospitality (cafés, restaurants, supermarkets);
- Tutoring, babysitting, or freelance gigs (where permitted);
- Internships related to your field of study (sometimes with additional work permissions).

Considerations and cautions

- Income expectations: Student jobs are typically minimum wage or slightly above. They can help with day-to-day costs but rarely cover tuition.
- Academic balance: Overworking can impact grades and health. Most universities recommend not exceeding 15–20 hours per week.

- Legal compliance: Working beyond permitted hours can breach visa conditions and lead to penalties or removal.
- Language barrier: In non-English-speaking countries, job opportunities may be limited to roles where local language skills are not essential.

Visa, residency and proof of funds

While tuition and scholarships are top of mind, visa and residency requirements can be equally important – and can often make or break an international application. From demonstrating financial readiness to understanding residency-linked fee structures, this section explains the essential rules you'll need to navigate.

Visa requirements: Financial proof

Most student visas require proof that you can support yourself throughout your studies. This is often a set amount calculated by the government based on expected living costs.

- Germany: Requires ~€10,332 (approx. £8,700) per year, held in a 'blocked account'.
- Canada: Must show funds for tuition plus CAD 10,000–15,000 (approx. £6,000–£9,000).
- United States: F-1 visa applicants must demonstrate full first-year funding.
- Australia: Must show access to around AUD 24,505 (approx. £13,000) for living costs. Following a 2024 policy change, Australia increased its required proof of funds for student visa applicants to AUD 29,710 (Reuters, 2024).
- Netherlands: Tuition + ~€12,000 (approx. £10,200) in living costs.
- Singapore: Financial documents proving you can meet tuition and living needs (typically SGD 10,000–12,000).

Check with the embassy or consulate for country-specific rules – and note that even fully funded scholarship holders may still need to show proof of personal savings.

Residency status and fee categories

In many countries, residency or nationality directly affects tuition fees:

- EU/EEA nationals pay reduced rates in the EU (or no tuition at all in Nordic countries).
- UK students post-Brexit may now pay international fees in many EU countries.
- Some countries offer 'domestic' fees to long-term residents or those with special visas (e.g. Green Card holders in the US).

Families should investigate whether a child's citizenship or dual nationality could provide eligibility for lower fees. However, advisers should warn families that some quite personal financial questions are often asked on forms when applying for local fees, for example, details of family income, savings or submission of tax returns/bank statements.

Post-arrival formalities

After arriving, students often need to:

- Register with immigration or local police (e.g. Germany, Spain).
- Open a local bank account.
- Maintain valid health insurance.
- Renew visas or residence permits annually.

These can carry added administrative and financial responsibilities – so it's worth budgeting time and money for them.

Plan ahead: Reassessment rare

Most universities won't reassess your aid package after admission. That means you should apply for all possible funding upfront and plan for future years.

It's also wise to check whether your visa or scholarship is renewable, and under what conditions (e.g. academic performance, maintaining full-time status).

Final thoughts

Studying abroad is a financial commitment – but it doesn't have to be out of reach. With careful research, early preparation and a clear understanding of costs and support, students from a wide range of backgrounds can access a world-class education. Affordability isn't just about choosing the cheapest option – it's about finding the best value, with the support to match.

Adviser checklist

Understand the full cost of attendance
- [x] Help families move beyond tuition headlines to consider total costs: living expenses, visa fees, insurance, travel, books and personal spending.

Compare options by country and subject
- [x] Use structured tables to highlight differences in tuition and living costs across major destinations, and by subject area.

Explain aid types clearly
- [x] Distinguish between merit-based, need-based and government or institutional aid. Clarify eligibility and sustainability of each.

Advise early action
☑ Encourage students to begin researching aid and scholarship deadlines in Year 12 or earlier. Most top scholarships have early deadlines.

Support strong applications
☑ Guide students on writing compelling scholarship essays and assembling documentation like financial statements and references.

Use reliable search tools
☑ Signpost students to trusted databases like Unifrog, ScholarshipPortal, IEFA, EducationUSA and DAAD.de.

Understand work rights
☑ Help students interpret work hour limits, permit rules and typical job types in each country. Flag risks of breaching visa terms.

Guide visa planning
☑ Support students in gathering financial documents and understanding proof-of-funds requirements for visa applications.

Clarify fee status
☑ Explain how residency, nationality or previous education may affect tuition fees. Some students may qualify for local rates.

Address equity and access
☑ Emphasise that funding exists for students from diverse backgrounds, and encourage all students to explore their options regardless of income.

Plan for the full degree
☑ Remind students to consider whether aid is renewable, whether costs rise annually and how to budget for the full course duration.

Highlight post-arrival responsibilities
☑ Make students aware of registration duties, bank accounts, insurance and the need to renew permits or aid annually.

Normalise conversations about money
☑ Create a safe space to talk about affordability, debt, family expectations and the practical realities of funding a degree abroad.

FURTHER INFORMATION

General scholarship databases and search tools

Source	Description	Link
Unifrog – Special Opportunities Tool	Tailored database for scholarships, summer schools and awards.	https://www.unifrog.org
ScholarshipPortal	EU-wide database of scholarships for international students.	https://www.scholarshipportal.com
DAAD (Germany)	Database of German government-funded and institutional scholarships.	https://www.daad.de/en/study-and-research-in-germany/scholarships
ScholarshipsCanada	Database of scholarships available to study in Canada.	https://www.scholarshipscanada.com
IEFA.org	International scholarship search tool, US and beyond.	https://www.iefa.org
EducationUSA	U.S. Department of State resource for international students.	https://educationusa.state.gov

Government and institutional scholarships

Scholarship/ Programme	Country	Link
DAAD Scholarships	Germany	https://www.daad.de/en/study-and-research-in-germany/scholarships
Australia Awards	Australia	https://www.dfat.gov.au/people-to-people/australia-awards
MEXT Scholarship	Japan	https://www.studyinjapan.go.jp/en/planning/scholarships/
Turing Scheme	UK	https://www.gov.uk/guidance/turing-scheme-apply-for-funding-for-international-placements
Erasmus+	EU/UK	https://erasmus-plus.ec.europa.eu
HK SAR Government Scholarship	Hong Kong	https://www.edb.gov.hk/en/index.html
Singapore Tuition Grant Scheme	Singapore	https://www.moe.gov.sg/financial-matters/awards-scholarships

Regional or country-specific awards

Programme	Eligible regions	Link
Belt and Road Scholarship (Hong Kong)	Asia (selected countries)	https://admissions.hku.hk/fees-and-scholarships/scholarships/belt-and-road-scholarship
APEC Scholarships	APEC economies	[Varies – consult individual universities or host countries]
Commonwealth Scholarships	Commonwealth countries	https://cscuk.fcdo.gov.uk

University-specific examples

Scholarship	Country	Link
President's Scholarship	Canada	https://www.ualberta.ca/en/admissions/tuition-and-scholarships/index.html (example: University of Alberta)
NUS Merit Scholarship	Singapore	https://www.nus.edu.sg/oam/scholarships

Athletic scholarships and sport bodies

Resource	Description	Link
NCAA Eligibility Center	For student-athletes applying to US universities	https://web3.ncaa.org/ecwr3

Work rights and visa guidance

Country or organisation	Resource	Link
UKCISA (UK visa and work guidance)	Visa/work rights for international students in the UK	https://www.ukcisa.org.uk
Study in Germany – Blocked Account and Proof of Funds	Financial requirements for German student visa	https://www.study-in-germany.de/en/plan-your-studies/requirements/proof-of-financial-resources_27533.php
Government of Canada – Study Permit	Proof of financial support for Canada	https://www.canada.ca/en.html
Australia Student Visa – Financial Capacity	Updated financial requirements (2024)	https://immi.homeaffairs.gov.au/
Netherlands Student Visa – IND	Living cost estimates and requirements	https://ind.nl/en
Singapore Student's Pass	Work conditions and financial proof	https://www.ica.gov.sg/

Conclusion: A journey shared, a future shaped

At the heart of every university application lies a young person standing at the threshold of possibility. This book has aimed to illuminate the path ahead – not with certainty, but with clarity. It is not only a guide to international admissions but a testament to what can be achieved when guidance is timely, informed and hopeful.

As we return to the spirit of the preface, it is fitting to recall the words of Rabindranath Tagore: *'Don't limit a child to your own learning, for he was born in another time.'* These words capture both the humility and vision that sit at the core of effective educational guidance. Our students do not walk the same paths we or their parents did, nor should they be confined by the limits of our understanding – the world is changing too fast for that. They deserve the freedom to explore, to falter, to flourish – across borders and expectations alike.

But we might also listen to a more recent voice – Malala Yousafzai, who reminds us:

'One child, one teacher, one book, one pen can change the world.' Said during a speech to the United Nations Youth Assembly on 12 July 2013 – her 16th birthday!

International education is more than a change of campus. For many, it is a key that unlocks opportunity. It offers access to institutions that value potential over pedigree, flexibility over formality and growth over grades. When understood well, it becomes a powerful lever for social mobility – not just moving students between countries, but lifting them beyond structural barriers and inherited limitations.

The stories shared throughout this book – from Nadia's unexpected path to Prague to Liz's quiet defiance in choosing literature over convention – remind us that there is no single route to success. What matters most is fit, not fame. Advisers who embrace this truth can transform moments of disappointment into chapters of renewal.

To support a student's international aspirations is to believe in their capacity to thrive beyond the familiar. It is to trust that with the right knowledge, encouragement and care, they will find their place in the world – not just as students, but as citizens shaped by diverse perspectives and common purpose.

May this guide serve not only as a manual, but as a quiet manifesto – one that insists that education, when made accessible and expansive, can be the most enduring passport of all.

As advisers, it's our responsibility – and our privilege – to help make these journeys possible: to open maps, highlight options and ensure that no student's future is limited by what they don't yet know.

Are you ready for the challenge?

NEW AND BESTSELLING FROM TROTMAN

Enhance your careers library with our bestsellers, visit: www.trotman.co.uk

www.ingramcontent.com/pod-product-compliance
Lightning Source LLC
Chambersburg PA
CBHW070334230426
43663CB00011B/2306